ON BECOMING COSMOPOLITAN

By Michael Yahuda

To dearest Daniella,
This is not a real autobiography.
I have written this in more of an
academic style. Nevertheless I hope
you will see it as representing
important developments in my life.
Much love, your Dad XX

Acknowledgements

I am immensely grateful to Amy Wooden who edited and prepared the book for publication and who could be relied upon for wise counsel and her professionalism.

Also, much gratitude is due to Kurt Foster for his encouragement and for his skill and patience in overcoming my manifold difficulties regarding both my computer and my printer.

I am deeply grateful to my colleague, Professor Robert Sutter, who took the time in his busy period of university examinations to read a draft of the book and for his generous and thoughtful comments. I am also grateful to Professor David Shambaugh for his comments on an earlier draft.

My former colleagues at the LSE and at the University of Southampton welcomed me unreservedly into their departments. They aided me in learning how to teach to different audiences and contributed greatly to my intellectual development, especially as I had no academic background in either Political Science or International Relations. In addition, I also benefitted much from having lively students and especially research students, who ended up knowing more about the subjects than I.

As always, I owe much to my third wife, Ellen, with whom I celebrated thirty years of marriage; she put-up with my changes of moods in the course of writing the book. She was always encouraging and willing to offer much needed support.

Finally, I am also grateful to my three children – Tamar, Daniella, and David – and my three granddaughters – Rachael, Omi, and Aisha – for reading a draft of the book. I owe a special thank you to Omi for offering very useful advice on improving the draft. My two stepchildren, Abigail and Matthew, welcomed me warmly as an addition to their family over thirty years ago when I first met Ellen, and their respective children – Emily, Hannah, and Nina and Jacob, Zach, and Eli – have treated me as if I were their real 'Granddad.'

Introduction: My Understanding of Cosmopolitanism

Cosmopolitanism is often contrasted with parochialism and narrow forms of nationalism. According to the Oxford Dictionary, a cosmopolitan is "a citizen of the world, one without national attachments or prejudices." In that sense, cosmopolitanism is the antithesis of nationalism. Nationalism (as opposed to patriotism, with which it has much in common) tends to emphasize the distinctiveness of a community – usually based on claims of shared ethnicity, land, history, culture, and language – to differentiate one specific nation from other nations, which are often regarded as inferior.

Jewish people are perhaps best known for being cosmopolitans since ancient times. Jewish communities existed in parts of the Roman empire well before they were expelled from the Land of Israel. That followed the destruction of their Temple in Jerusalem in AD 70 and at least two rebellions, the last in 130. Despite being dispersed among many parts of the world, the Jews retained their religious, ethnic, and cultural identities – even as other ancient neighboring peoples lost theirs. They lived as often-persecuted peoples among other nations for almost two thousand years, until the establishment of the state of Israel in 1948. They may therefore be regarded as the first cosmopolitans. With the establishment of Christianity as the official religion of Rome in the early 4th Century, Jews began to experience being considered as deviants from the true religion and as so-called "Christ Killers". Persecution of Jews became widespread in Christian Europe in the Middle Ages. The Moslems, however, tolerated the Jews until the modern era, albeit as people of lesser status. Indeed, they played an important role in the flourishing of the roots of modernity in Spain and Portugal (Andalusia).

Building on the religious persecution of Jews in earlier periods in Christian Europe, Jews suffered from discrimination in the nationalistic periods of the 19th and 20th centuries. Before the establishment of Israel as a state to which Jews could migrate to escape persecution, Jews were attacked as "rootless cosmopolitans" by the Nazis. In contrast, before the twentieth century, there was a tolerance for Jews in the Arab and Moslem worlds, albeit as a people with lesser status than Moslems, but they began to come under attack with the advent of nationalism in the Arab world.

Arguably, the enmity between Israel and the Palestinian Arabs can be understood in terms of modern nationalism, as a clash between two peoples over land rights. In the current era of globalization and 'anti globalists', Stephen Miller, a close adviser to former President Trump, has used the term cosmopolitan in that pejorative sense to criticize alleged "globalists", i.e., so-called elitists supposedly detached from citizens of their own countries.

I like to think of myself as a cosmopolitan person, primarily as a result of lifetime experiences. I am a citizen of three countries (Britain, Israel, and America), and I feel degrees of patriotism towards each of them, while at the same time being critical of some of their respective politics and cultures. For some sixty years I have been immersed in the study and teaching of Chinese and East Asian politics, without having a personal or emotional connection with any Asian country.

I have nothing in common with depictions of cosmopolitans as "elitist globalists", supposedly detached from their fellow citizens and patriots. On the contrary, I have a strong feeling of place, even though, like most people in the world today, I have multiple identities and loyalties. For example, as an academic I share a commitment to the values of my profession with other academics in all parts of the world and have a particular affinity with fellow students of Chinese politics and International Relations, even though I do not necessarily share their views. I also share a sense of community with those who live in my neighborhood, as well as with those who live within my federal state of Maryland and beyond that to America as a nation, of which I am proud to be a citizen. In addition, I have strong patriotic feelings towards England and Israel.

But contrary to those who think that as a "citizen of the world" I should feel an obligation to treat or regard all others as equals, I feel, like most people, closest to the members of my family, to whom I have varying degrees of obligation. As with many contemporary people, the members of my family live in more than one country. What makes me identify myself as a cosmopolitan is the fact that I have grown up and lived in several countries, absorbed their diverse cultures, while also having immersed myself in the histories, politics, and cultural traditions of China and other Asian cultures. As a result, I think I have an understanding and a tolerance for many diverse ways of thinking about people's views of others and of their respective places in the world.

My parents, who met by chance soon after the Second World War was declared, could not have been more different. My father came from a highly distinguished Jewish family in Jerusalem, which could trace its origins to the Babylonian diaspora, more than 2500 years ago. My mother, who was 12 years older than he, came from a Christian family in Christchurch, New Zealand. My father was not a practicing Jew, but he was very proud of being Jewish. My mother was a convinced atheist. I don't know of any specific agreement between my parents about my religious upbringing, but as far as I can remember, I always thought of myself as being Jewish without having the faintest idea of what that meant before the age of nine, when we migrated to Israel. However, even as a child in London in the 1940s, I felt different from others in my class and from my playmates – even though in nearly all respects our lives were similar.

As I look back over life from the age of 80, I am conscious of thinking about my identity as a person of feelings, beliefs, and associations which have accumulated over time and yet seemingly always have been a part of me. I am aware that my memories of events in my youth, like those of others, are unreliable as accurate representations of my past, especially for an older person looking back on my childhood and adolescence. My remembrances of particular episodes may have been distorted by my own current preferences or prejudices, or they may be remembered as a result of having heard them retold by my parents and affected by their perspectives. Consequently, my remembered past may no longer be faithful depictions of actual events as I saw them at the time. Nevertheless, like others, I have been influenced – and perhaps my character shaped – by the images I carry with me of those distant events and childhood experiences. In addition, I have most likely been shaped by influences and experiences in my earlier years of which I am but dimly aware or have been buried in my subconscious.

I was born in Hampstead, north London, in 1940 and spent the early war years in a nursery run by Anna Freud, the daughter of the great man, and my late father used to maintain that facets of my character were formed by that experience. But I have no memory at all of the nursery, or of Anna Freud, the founder of child psychoanalysis, and cannot say anything about how the experience may or may not have affected my subsequent development.

It is part of human nature to try and make sense of our surroundings, experiences, and what we have seen. Whatever the narratives we weave about them, or whatever the explanations we may advance, these are rarely constant, as they evolve over time to take into account new developments or further reflections. Consequently, my understandings of how I, as an older person, came to think of what has shaped my identity has doubtlessly changed over the years in ways I cannot fully recognize. Yet, at each stage in my development through life, I have held my respective visions of myself to be true at the time. We have all been influenced in numerous ways by our parents, our views of them, and of how they brought us up. But my views of them and the character of my relationships with them – and indeed with each of them as individuals, as I shall elaborate in the next chapter – has changed greatly over the course of the thirty years or so since their deaths. In fact, I have grown to appreciate them more with the passage of time. However much my reflections on how I came to be the person I believe I am may have changed in the course of my 80 years, there is no way of my knowing which of these visions is more reflective of what may be said to be my core identity. However, I believe, of course, that my current view is the most significant.

In my case, it is no exaggeration to say that my life as an adult was determined in the main by my experiences and by decisions made by my parents. Having taken me away on the eve of my 9th birthday from a settled and on the whole a happy life in London, my parents took me to Israel in 1949. After initial problems of adjustment, when I was teased as 'a little Englishman,' I virtually assimilated as a young Israeli at one of the country's best schools. However, in order that their only child should escape military service, my parents yanked me off back to dismal London just before my 16th birthday in 1956, where I no longer knew anyone. After a year of living with my mother, who returned to Israel to be with my father, I was then left alone in a boarding house at the age of 17 for most of my second year there. By September 1959, I had enrolled as a student at London University. Some months later, I felt duty bound to marry my first-ever girl friend, as she was pregnant. During those three years since leaving Israel, I had received no guidance, let alone advice, from my parents. Perhaps the one good thing I did in those three years was to decide to study for a degree in Chinese at London University, which was to open the door to a rewarding academic career for me.

To the best of my recollections, I had a happy childhood in London, but, looking back from the present vantage point, I can see there were problems of which I was unaware at the time. My father was the youngest son of a highly orthodox and notable Jerusalem family, whose grandfather had moved there in the mid-19th century from Baghdad. My father had come to London to study law at University College and, like his friends, he was a committed Zionist. My mother was a tourist from New Zealand, who was in Germany when war was declared and left for London, as British subjects were instructed by the embassy to go "home". In those days, New Zealanders were brought up to think of Britain as home. My parents met by chance at a boarding house in south Hampstead in London and my mother was immediately courted by my father, even though she was not a Jew and was twelve years older than he. I was born in late September 1940. They had married in a registry office on April 1st (the date was concealed from me from me until I was well into my twenties). My mother's family was Christian and she was a firm atheist. I suppose, given my father's Jewish pedigree, no one would have questioned my Jewishness at that time. My father was a non-observant Jew, but very proud of his ancestry and of his identity as a Jew. I was brought up to think of myself as a Jew, but was told little about it. In any event I was sent to a local Church of England primary school. The Passover dinner was the only Jewish event that was celebrated at home. We also celebrated Christmas like most English families.

At the time, none of this bothered me. In most respects, I was not readily distinguishable from other boys in the neighborhood, but a small part of me did feel different. My father instilled in me a sense that I was the scion of a famous Jewish family. I suddenly had a vivid demonstration of this when I was seven years old. My father had a highly distinguished uncle, Abraham Shalom Yahuda, who was an acclaimed professor of Semitic studies, and an associate of famous people. My father had quarreled with his uncle, when he had been in his care in the 1930s, and the two broke contact with each other. But after the war, when my father heard his uncle had moved to a house near us, he sought to resume relations. As we shall see later, relations were sundered still further.

As mentioned earlier, I have lived in three countries, each of which, at the time, I expected to be my permanent home. These were successively England, Israel, back to England, and, since 2003, the United States. I am deeply attached to each without feeling that any one of them has a prior claim on my loyalty. As a secular Jew, with a Jewish father and a non-Jewish mother, I feel strongly attached to Jewish history and culture. Like the former Israeli Prime Minister, Golda Meir, I think, "it was not God who chose the Jews, but rather the Jews who chose God" over 2500 years ago. Since then, the Law has guided them. Unlike most other faiths, Jews do not openly proclaim belief in their god. Their prayers, songs, psalms, poems, and incantations are devoted to the praise of god and requests for his blessings. An orthodox Jew is required to follow 613 commandments (or Mitzvot), which govern every aspect of his/her life. As noted earlier, Jews, since ancient times, have been dispersed throughout the world as minority communities amidst much more numerous, often-hostile peoples. Unlike nearly all of their ancient contemporaries, they have survived as a distinct community of peoples, bound by ancient precepts, sustained in large part by the hope or belief that they would return one day to live in their holy land. As they say at every Passover festival, "next year in Jerusalem". In that sense, I am a Zionist and an upholder of the righteousness of the existence of the state of Israel, but not necessarily the policies of its various governments since 1948.

At the same time, I recognize the legitimacy of the claims of Palestinian Arabs to statehood. In the terminology of contemporary international relations, two separate nations claim the same territory for their respective states. In other words, like the late Amos Oz, I adhere to a "two state solution". But for that to come about, it requires both nations, or peoples, to accept the legitimacy of the claims of the other. Unfortunately, that is far from the case at the present time. Meanwhile, there is no reason why the two sets of peoples should not respect and find inspiration in the diverse cultures of the other. After all, in the different forms of their faiths and beliefs all regard the Patriarch Abraham as one of their founding fathers. Indeed, before the advent of modern nationalism, Jews and Arabs drew much from their respective cultures, especially in the golden era of Moslem Spain in the 10th and 12th centuries, when they combined to make significant contributions in fields as extensive as science, medicine, philosophy, literature, and art. In fact, my father's uncle, who attended the first five Zionist Congresses beginning in 1897, argued strongly over thirty years before his death in 1951 that the Zionist establishment ignored the Andalusian dimension of the Jewish tradition to the detriment of relations with the Arab world. Nevertheless, my great uncle was honored in Israel with a state funeral.

Having spent my childhood, my late teens and most of my adult life in England, including notably 30 fascinating years as an academic at the London School of Economics, I have a deep affection for the country and its extraordinary variety of people. My parents were an unusual couple. My father was the youngest child of eight. His father, Isaac, (my paternal grandfather) belonged to a highly distinguished Jewish family that migrated from Baghdad in 1853 to become one of the leading families of that community in Jerusalem. I was brought up in London, in a largely secular environment, although my father made a point of stressing our identity as Jews, i.e., his and mine. My mother, however, firmly insisted on her identity as a confirmed atheist, and she too was a strong influence on my development and had claims on my loyalty. Perhaps their combined influence may account for my having been something of an outsider for most of my life, who yet happily played a part in social groups in a non-rebellious way.

A more intellectual reason that has come to sustain my cosmopolitanism is the recognition that the nation and state have become too narrow a basis for our loyalty and that in some respects that loyalty can run counter to our interests and perhaps even to our long-term survival. We live in a world of over 200 nation-states, whose governments are supposedly chosen by the people (i.e., citizens) to represent their best interests. State governments are supposedly accountable to the people they represent. But states and their peoples do not live in isolation, and, in the modern and contemporary periods, peoples of the various states have become more closely interconnected. Governments have found it increasingly difficult to oversee, let alone control, these interconnections, which extend from economics, to personal interactions among people of diverse nations. Contemporary people throughout the world participate in the continuous development of technologies, take part in the free flow of ideas, and share in the problems caused by the rapid changes in the global environment.

Our means of dealing with these interconnections are not only inefficient, but they are so dependent on statehood as to be self-defeating. Take for example, the issue of climate change (perhaps the most important issue confronting our existence on the planet). We are not organized globally to address it properly. We rely on voluntary agreements between states (or rather the governments of states), who alone have the capacity to marshal the resources necessary to address this immense challenge. In order to deal with the effects of climate change the peoples of small and less developed states have fewer capabilities than those of larger and more developed states. Not only are the less capable dependent on the more capable to take their interests into account in the making of relevant policies, but in order to do so larger states may find that in the process of helping others they will hurt the interests of their own people, or particular sectors of them – at least in the short term. Take India, as an example, because of its huge and growing population it must develop and grow its economy, if it is to meet the basic needs of its people, hundreds of millions of whom live at near subsistence levels. Its government is democratically answerable to its citizens, but not to those of less developed small states, whose very existence may be threatened by India's extensive use of coal. Thus by its energy policies to meet the needs of its own people, it threatens others.

The United Nations and its various agencies cannot help much, as it's an organization of states. Yet even the UN Charter allows for the recognition of the human rights of individuals, as well as the rights of states. However, it is the rights of states that have predominated in practice. We need to think and act in broader terms than those of the governments of states, whose primary responsibilities are to serve the immediate interests of their own peoples. On some issues, states have agreed to cede some authority to supra-state organizations, such as the World Health Organization (WHO) or the World Trade Organization (WTO). In addition to monitoring outbreaks of especially contagious diseases, the WHO seeks to enforce international norms and organize multiple actors to treat outbreaks. But ultimately it is dependent on the cooperation of states and on their ability to maintain domestic order in affected areas. The WTO regulates international trade and has the legal authority to adjudicate disputes, but it, too, is ultimately dependent on the cooperation of states. Although the main trade actors are multi-national companies, trade statistics are usually presented as trade between states. In other words, as in the case of many international organizations, the principal power and authority are exercised by states. That still leaves open a niche role for non-governmental organizations (NGOs) and International NGOs.

There is a clear disconnect with the state-centered international organizations and the increasingly global character of many pressing issues. Climate change may be the most pressing and the most difficult challenge. Crucial states such as China, India, Russia and the United States are unlikely to cede sovereignty to a global body to enable it to address the issue effectively. These and other state governments will only respond if effective pressure is brought to bear on them through public opinion, commercial interests, new technological developments and other forms of persuasion. The same applies to other issues that need to be addressed globally, or by cross state means, such as the sharing of river waters and the appropriate management of other natural resources.

Immense bureaucratic difficulties would have to be surmounted to overcome state and sovereignty objections to what would amount to a ceding of even some of their authority to new kinds of universal organizations of uncertain provenance and accountability. It would take a great deal of time to bring about such a major change of organizations. Meanwhile it is important to raise the level of popular awareness of the significance of cosmopolitanism, as opposed to nationalism. At a global or universal level, Nationalism is divisive, separating the interests of states and their peoples from each other. Cosmopolitanism, by contrast, allows for and indeed encourages the recognition of common interests and affinities, which is the only way a universalist approach and organization can be brought together to address these global problems.

The current intensity of nationalism and populism in many countries around the world has been seen as a counter to globalism. As a result, globalization is perceived to threaten the identities of communities and nations. The current aversion to cosmopolitanism, which is seen as the prerogative of global elites divorced from the lives of ordinary people, is

13

an obstacle to deal with current threats, which do not stem from interstate rivalries as before. However, as noted earlier, nationalism, or perhaps its milder form of patriotism (love of country) need not be thought of as the counterpart of cosmopolitanism. Love of one's own country can be extended to others, not necessarily with the same passion and intensity, but sufficient to have an appreciation for and an understanding of other peoples and their cultures. Indeed, a patriot of one country and its people may even have a sense of empathy for others.

Ideally, it is to be hoped that at some point there may be a movement for primary and secondary schools to incorporate degrees of cosmopolitanism in their curricula. But the obstacles to that happening are immense. In particular it would encounter resistance from most governments who, necessarily, seek through education to inculcate pride in one's country, its national history, its institutions and the values, which underpin them. Yet in a world where the most existential threats to human life are increasingly of a global kind, rather than traditional interstate warfare, the importance of cultivating a cosmopolitan outlook could not be graver.

The succeeding chapters will follow the evolution of my life, as it shaped my development as a cosmopolitan, with a concluding chapter stressing the growing significance of cosmopolitanism.

Chapter 1: From London to Tel-Aviv

Most people have multiple political identities and loyalties as they relate to their immediate families; their local communities; and their respective nation states. To these may be added as appropriate, ethnic, religious, professional, and other identities. Indeed, a self-consciousness of possessing different identities maybe one of the defining characteristics of modernity resulting from greater connectivity between people and places.

In my case the issue of identity is complicated by my experiences growing up in two different countries, beginning with a childhood in London, then my early teens in Israel, and my return to London in 1956 at the age of sixteen. I spent the following sixty plus years as a student, teacher, researcher, and writer on a totally unrelated geographical region of East Asia with its divergent cultures. More specifically, I was born in 1940 in London, where I spent my childhood until just before my 9ᵗʰ birthday, when I was whisked off to Israel, where I became for all intents and purposes an Israeli adolescent. Needless to say, I did not enjoy leaving Israel for dismal London in the summer of 1956, but I knuckled down to my studies and duly qualified for entrance to university in 1959, when I embarked on a degree in Modern Chinese Language and Literature. This led me to pursue an academic career in Chinese politics and the international relations of the Asia-Pacific. In other words, I passed through a relatively happy childhood in 1940s England to become a joyful Israeli in my teens in the 1950s before becoming a lonely studious young Englishman, who felt something of an outsider in my early twenties.

As mentioned earlier, I like to think of myself as a cosmopolitan person, initially because of a lifetime of experiencing different cultures and emotional attachments. But also because my academic life, spanning more than sixty years, has been directed towards studying countries with cultures wholly different from my own. Nor have I had personal or familial connections with any Asian country. With such a wide range of experiences of living in very different countries and having been exposed to varieties of ways of thought, I feel myself tolerant of divergent view points and interested in trying to understand better their provenance and implications. That is not to say I do not have viewpoints and commitments of my own, some of which are deeply felt, but these have been enriched by recognizing the significance of others.

I do not see cosmopolitans as "elitist globalists". Needless to say, I am not "rootless", as anti-Semites have defamed Jews, but neither am I a "citizen of the world", which is one of the definitions of a cosmopolitan. To the contrary, I have strong feeling of place, even though, as most people in the world today, I have multiple identities and loyalties. For example, as an academic I share a commitment to the values of my profession with academics in all parts of the world and have a particular affinity with fellow students of Chinese politics and International Relations, including both those who are Chinese and those who are not. I also share a sense of community with those who live within my federal state of Maryland and beyond that to Americans as a nation and the U.S.A., as a state of which I am proud to be a citizen. Like many people in the world today – and especially the young in Europe – I share a sense of community with many like-minded people in other countries, while also being a citizen of each of my adopted countries.

Contrary to those who think that as a "citizen of the world", I should feel an obligation to treat or to regard all others equally, I feel, like most people, closest to members of my family to whom I have varying degrees of obligation. Like many contemporary people, the members of my family live in more than one country. What contributes to my thinking of myself is the fact that I have grown up and lived in several countries, absorbed much of their diverse cultures, while also having immersed myself in the histories, politics and cultural traditions of China and other Asian cultures. As a result, I think I have an understanding and a tolerance for the cultures and thoughts of others.

My parents have been a major influence in shaping my life, but not always in ways they or I appreciated at the time. However, even as a child in London in the 1940s, I felt different from my fellow classmates and friends, even though in nearly all other respects our lives were similar. My father studied law at University College London, when in late Autumn 1939 he visited one of his Zionist friends in South Hampstead and, as family legend has it, he looked up from the entrance hall to see a woman – whom he had never seen before – crossing a landing on the floor above. He turned to his friend saying, "Do you see that woman up there? I am going to marry her". He was then 25 and she 37. She had left New Zealand (which was then a far more distant and isolated country than it is today) a few months earlier in 1939. She traveled by ship, determined to see Europe. Her ship had taken her through South Asia, the Middle East to Italy, and then to Germany. She was having a merry time in Berlin, when suddenly on September 3 war was declared and the British embassy called on all British subjects to "return home". As any New Zealander in those days, she had been brought up to think of Britain as home, and so she immediately went to London, where she was enthralled to see Whitehall, Piccadilly, and all the other famous sites that were household names in distant New Zealand. Through a chance acquaintance, she went to stay at the same boarding house where my father visited his friend.

My father, true to his word, pursued and courted my mother, and in due course she became pregnant. Being more pragmatic than her headstrong yet impulsive suitor, my mother refused to marry him and retreated to the Welsh resort of Mumbles to have her baby as a single mother. That had become more feasible at that time, because the government had made various arrangements to help single mothers work and care for their children, as the fathers were away on wartime duty. In any event, my father pursued her there and they were married at the Hampstead registry office on April 1, 1940 – an anniversary they tried to hide from me for two decades, evidently, they were embarrassed to have conceived me out of wedlock. I was born on September 29. What made the whole episode remarkable, was less the fact that my mother was almost 12 years older than my father and that she gave birth at the age of 38 (which was highly unusual in those days) than the fact that my father was a member of one of the most highly esteemed Babylonian Jewish families in Jerusalem. His father, Isaac Ezekiel Yahuda, was a scholar of international repute of Judaica and Arabica, who corresponded with the Vatican, and who was consulted on Islamic law by the center of studies of Islamic law at Al Azhar University in Cairo. He was a very observant Jew, and I am sure it would never have occurred to him that his son would "marry out" and provide him with a grandson the orthodox could not recognize as Jewish. Apparently, my father telegrammed to inform my grandfather of my birth and, as none of his other seven children had produced a boy to carry on the family name, my grandfather died a few months later a happy man.

My father, who apparently thought norms and rules did not apply to him, tried to keep my lack of orthodox Jewish credentials secret. After all, who in Jewish circles would have thought a member of such a distinguished family would be lacking in that regard? My mother did not give up her atheism, nor did she draw attention to it. I suppose her public silence was an early version of "don't ask, don't tell". In any event, I was duly circumcised by the leading mohel in London, Dr. Snowman, who was later to circumcise Prince Charles. I was brought up to think of myself as a Jew, but was told little about it. I was sent to a local Church of England primary school, where I remember once being chased around the playground as a "dirty little Jew". My pursuers were stopped and reprimanded by the school caretaker, a Mr. Weaver, and there the matter rested, as I never heard anything further about the incident.

The Passover dinner was the only Jewish event celebrated at home, with my father taking the part of leader and conducting the occasion as his father had done before him. The Passover was conducted in Hebrew, which neither my mother nor I understood, and it lasted for about three hours. Otherwise, we celebrated Christmas like most English families, with a Christmas tree, a roasted turkey, and presents.

In most respects, I was not readily distinguishable from other boys in the neighborhood, but as noted earlier a small part of me did feel different. My father instilled in me a sense that I was the scion of an eminent Jewish family. I suddenly had a vivid demonstration of this when I was seven years old. As noted earlier, my father had a famous uncle, Abraham Shalom Yahuda, who was an acclaimed scholar of Semitic studies. My father had quarreled with him, when he had been in his uncle's care in the 1930s and the two broke contact with each other. The uncle had a house in London in Elsworthy Road, N.W.3, not far from where we lived in Merton Rise, to which he had returned from America not long after the end of the War.

My father thought this was an opportunity to mend their relationship. He baked a marzipan cake, which was a favorite of the uncle and sent me in my 'Sunday suit' to deliver it to him. I trotted down the road with the cake perched on my outstretched hands and then pulled the old-fashioned bell at the top of the stairs to the house. A huge man in a black waist-coated suit opened the door and, thinking that he was the uncle, I began to address him in accordance with my instructions. He quickly stopped me and, calling me "sir" asked me to wait as he retreated behind the front door. Suddenly an even bigger man dressed in a suit with tails appeared and with a sour look on his face, which had a big wart near his mouth, looked down at me and asked me, "What do you want?" I responded with my well- rehearsed statement, "I am Michael Benjamin Yahuda, the son of Benjamin Jacob Yahuda, who has specially baked this cake for you". Looking down at me, he said, "Give it to me", which I did, and the uncle then promptly went inside the house closing the door, leaving me outside. I was secretly delighted, as I was afraid that this imposing great man would invite me in and ask me all kinds of questions. I skipped back home to tell my waiting father all that had transpired, with all the details I could remember.

A few days later my father's older brother, Joseph, whom I had never seen before and who, like my father, was a barrister, came to our house with a big white five-pound note for me from 'the uncle'. My father immediately told his brother, Joseph, to take it back, who responded by saying that it was not my father's right to refuse. My father then sent him on his way with the repost that as I was still a minor, he had every right to refuse to accept it. The result was that not only did my father fail to remake contact with his uncle, but he also broke relations with his eldest brother for the next ten years.

Meanwhile, I had come to think of New Zealand as a land of plenty. My mother's parents had died several years before I was born, but she kept in contact with her sisters, despite the long time it took to exchange letters. During the War, we received occasional food parcels from my mother's sisters and cousins that became more regular once peace had been restored, because we were still subject to rationing. One of her nephews popped in to see us after he was de-mobbed at the end of the war, and I was impressed by my 'cousin Bob' in his uniform and by the pleasant way in which he treated my parents. This was a time of austerity in

England, which I remember from receiving food parcels, including boxes of oranges, from my father's sisters in Jerusalem. My memory of "VE Day" (the Victory in Europe Day) is of sitting on my father's shoulders at the back of Buckingham Palace as an endless stream of armored vehicles and tanks carrying soldiers in green uniforms went by. People all around were cheering like mad, but I got bored after a while, and we went home.

Despite the general austerity and the slow recovery caused by the devastation from the War and the beginnings of the retreat from Empire, the early post-War years were a happy time for me. We lived in a rented two bedroom flat with a separate kitchen and bathroom. We also had access to the garden, which was mainly weeds and grass – an ideal playground for my friends and me. Our flat was on the first floor of a four-story house built for the middle classes in the early 20th century. The flat was within easy walking distance of Primrose Hill, with Regents Park just beyond that. My friends and I happily played there, and I fell in love with cricket, especially after being taken to Lords Cricket Ground where I saw my boyhood hero, Dennis Compton, play for England against the visiting New Zealanders.

I spent most Saturday mornings at the local Odeon cinema, which had special programs for children, with cartoons, cowboy films, and series such as Batman and Superman. However, I was not a great fan of those comic book heroes, who single handedly would save helpless citizens from evildoers. Paradoxically, that did not bother me when it came to cowboy films, where the heroes were also lone cowboys, who would ride out by themselves into the sunset. As for comic books, I much preferred the irreverent humor of British ones such as, The Beano, with characters such as Dennis the Menace, Lord Snooty, and Gnasher. We boys also had great fun playing imaginary games in the remains of Anderson shelters against wartime bombing.

My most vivid memories of War were of nearly being bombed in our house. I must have been about four, when my mother rushed me out of the kitchen to hide under the stairs nearby as the thud-like noise of a "Doodlebug" (a German V-1 rocket) passed overhead and my mother urged it to continue its journey, for when the noise of its engine stopped, the rocket would plunge to earth with its deadly explosives. My second and even more vivid memory is of a terrible explosion in the middle of the night as the shutters and taped glass of our windows flew all over the bedroom and onto my bed. It was a supersonic and more deadly V-2 rocket that had destroyed two houses just a block away. My mother refused to take shelter from the bombing. There were reports of people being trapped in bomb-shelters, and the conditions in the underground train stations – where many people sought shelter – were dirty and noisy. She took the practical view that there was no guarantee against being bombed even in shelters, and, as our neighborhood had not been subject to saturation bombing, it was better to stay in our clean home. I think her calm and rational approach to danger influenced me greatly in subsequent years. I don't recall ever being overcome by feelings of panic and anxiety.

Chapter 2: Formative Years in Israel

One day in the spring of 1949, my parents suddenly announced that my father would leave for the newly founded state of Israel and prepare for our joining him there in the autumn. It was with great excitement that I located Israel (actually Palestine under the British UN Mandate) on the world atlas at school that was largely covered in the pinkish red of the British Empire, and my schoolteacher spoke of a Holy Land of sun and palm trees. That September I had my first insight into the enormity of the undertaking on which we had embarked, as I saw elderly people weeping as their younger families were taking their leave to board the boat train at Waterloo station. My mother explained that they did not think they would ever see each other again.

We crossed the Chanel that night and stayed a few days in Paris. To my mother's delight, the shops were full with all different cuts of meat and every kind of cheese. Brought up on the thin gruel of rationing, it was all too much for me and I'm afraid I deeply disappointed my mother, who for the first time in a good many years came face to face with the abundance of food which New Zealand had to offer, only to find it rejected by her one and only son.

During the journey by boat from Marseille to Haifa, I threw all my cricket gear into the sea after learning from the ship's mechanic that the game wasn't played in Israel. I now see it as a gesture symbolizing my break with England. We duly reached the port of Haifa a few days later, where I was astonished to see people from the ship getting on their knees on embarkation to kiss the ground.

After a night with my father's brother Solomon in Haifa, We then stayed for about two months with my father's sister, Reina, in Tel-Aviv. My mother and I found it so hot we were able to bathe in the sea till late November, even though the locals thought us crazy. By the New Year, we had moved to a new settlement for immigrants called Hadar Yosef, some five miles away. It was a network of two-story concrete blocks with each containing four single-bedroom apartments on the ground floor and two double-bedroom ones on the floor above with a flat roof on top. Others were still being built when we moved to a two-bedroom apartment overlooking an abandoned orange grove. Our apartment had two bedrooms and was equipped with basic provisions: a kitchen, running cold water, a toilet and a shower room, electricity, and an icebox. The floors of the rooms were tiled and the walls white washed. I had a small room to myself, which I came to recognize was considered a luxury by others. We had a large garden running along one side of the house.

Once my parents and I had cleared away the sand and builder's rubbish to a depth of about a foot, we found good earth on which my parents grew vegetables and flowers. Israel too was experiencing austerity and rationing, but unlike London there was an optimistic air, as people were sure that with hard work, conditions would improve. My parents built a chicken coop in the garden, which they fenced to keep out foxes. We had our own supply of eggs and chickens. Three years later, my father set up a loft on the roof for homing pigeons.

Hadar Yosef was nevertheless a rough and ready place. When we first looked out of our back-window, which faced the orange grove, we saw a family of jackals strolling by. Although we subsequently came across foxes, including a beautiful silver one, we never saw the jackals again. I suppose the pace at which houses were being built left no room for such creatures. Beyond the orange trees was a hill with the remains of a few Arab houses, which were known as Sheikh Mounis. A few years later, after I left in 1956; and as Tel-Aviv expanded, the whole area was built up as an upscale suburb called Ramat-Aviv.

Jewish migrants, or rather displaced people from all over the world populated Hadar Yosef. In the adjoining apartment to us was a family from Poland with two boys, one my age and the other, three years older. They had tattooed numbers on their arms from Nazi concentration camps and had managed to escape with

27

their parents on a long trek to Israel via Turkey. The four single-bedroom apartments on the floor below us were occupied respectively by a Bulgarian couple, a Hungarian couple (a young opera singer and her mother), and a German family, who managed to build a small blacksmith facility in the backyard. In the house opposite to us was a family from Egypt with a woman who suffered from elephantiasis. In short, the neighborhood was a polyglot of people, the like of whom I had never seen before, all speaking strange, foreign languages. Hadar Yosef opened up a whole new world to me. The local shoe repairer specialized in stitching bits of leather to repair broken shoes or sandals. A middle-aged man explained to me how he had chosen his wife, because her kitchen pantry was full of food – the like of which he had never seen before.

My favorite memory is of Max, a man in his thirties, who had a character that was larger than life. His love of adventure and passion for life made him extraordinarily attractive to me as a young boy. He was of Lithuanian origin from South Africa. He had enlisted at the start of the war by lying about his age and belonged to the South African contingent that went overland to North Africa. He got bored while stationed in Cairo and stole his commander's car to use as a taxi. Towards the end of the war, he found himself stationed in Italy in charge of a military gas (or petrol) station, which he used as a source for private funds. He was one of the few men I have ever encountered who enjoyed the chaos of warfare, and he came to Israel to participate in the war of independence. In fact, at one point, his wife had to rush to the airport to stop him from enlisting for the war in Korea. He was barely literate, yet he worked for the Ministry of Education as a driver who took educational material to

Arab villages in northern Galilee. On one occasion he took me with him, and we had a whale of time. Although he spoke no Arabic and his Hebrew was idiosyncratic, he got on well with the Arab communities we visited, and we were treated to endless cups of Turkish coffee, Baklava, and other Arab cakes and sweets.

None of my contemporaries spoke English, but Hebrew was beginning to be spoken by the young. I was sent to the local school, where I picked up Hebrew in no time. My parents and I were regarded as oddballs. Most of our fellow migrants would have given their eye teeth to have been able to migrate to England and yet we who, by their standards, were well-off in London had chosen to give it all up for the poorer living conditions and the uncertainties of life in Israel. My father, who had a law degree from London University and who had practiced law in England, was restarting as a lawyer in reduced circumstances in an immigrants' settlement outside Tel-Aviv. I was later to learn that in his late teens and early twenties he had served as the assistant to his distinguished father, whose eyesight was failing. As his father's representative, he had dealt with the notables of the day, including Israel's premier poet, Nahman Bialik, leading Zionist politicians, including Yitzhak Ben Zvi (a subsequent President of the country) and Yigal Allon (an army general and labor leader) among many others. Yet on his return after the War of Independence, my father found no patronage or preference. The many talents he had to offer as a professional man of learning and a speaker of eight languages, including Arabic, were ignored.

As a nine-year old, I knew little of this. I was caught up in the youthful enthusiasm to contribute to building the country in the spirit of the pioneers who struggled in the early years of the Kibbutzim and who had won the war of independence of 1948 against all odds. My only discomfort was that I was called the "Englishman", especially as at the beginning my Hebrew was characterized by an English accent, unlike everyone else at school. Indeed, one of my schoolteachers took against me that first year. Like many others in Hadar Yosef, he was from Poland. He used to punish me in class. On one occasion he hit me with a ruler and sent me home (which was within easy walking distance). It so happened my father was home and on hearing my story, he grabbed my hand and dragged me to the school. Bursting into the classroom where the teacher had not yet finished the class, my father confronted him, told him of my supposed prowess at my school in London and pointing into his face told the cowering teacher if he dared to lay a finger on me again my father would throw him out of the window. I was mortified and hoped in vain that the ground would open up and swallow me. It didn't, but it became clear that I could no longer attend that school.

I was then taken to be interviewed by the head master, Mr. Bograshov, of the most famous school in Israel, Gymnasia Herzelia. The school was the first modem Jewish school in the country, and it could be said that Tel-Aviv was built around it. Many of those who were to become the elite of Israel were educated there. The headmaster, who interviewed me, knew my grandfather and had met my father, so to no-one's surprise I gained admission. My six years there turned out to be perhaps the happiest of my young life. I used to ride most days on my bicycle the five miles to school early in the morning and return often in the heat of the day after lunch or sometimes stay on and go to the beach or to the swimming pool on the way home.

Studying came easily to me and I was able to join in all the games and sports of my classmates. The School had a policy of leading us on hikes and, later, on trips of several days and nights to get to know the country. With others, I also participated in youthful pre-army camps. In particular, I enjoyed one that was connected with the Air Force, where I excelled in the mathematics of aerodynamics and in the making of model planes from balsa-wood. Had I stayed on in the country, I would probably have enlisted in the Air Force to become a pilot.

At least that was my dream at the age of 15. The friendships I made at school were deep and long lasting. Over fifty years later, in 1999, they sought me out for the fiftieth class-reunion, when I met up again with my girlfriend from my teens and two of my closest friends from when I was fifteen. It was as if the intervening five decades had dropped off without trace, and, as one of them put it, we had become "old new friends".

Even though I was a happy and a relatively privileged Israeli youth, I became increasingly aware of shadows appearing over Israeli society and the deepening of certain problems. The earlier appeal of the non-materialist communal living as represented by the kibbutz movement was becoming outmoded as the ideal for a more complex urban society which was rapidly emerging. Even in the relatively sheltered Gymnasia Herzelia, our class was divided between the "kibbutzniks" and the "salonists". The former, in the spirit of the pioneers, wanted to be fighters and farmers. They hoped to join NAHAL (the acronym for young fighters and farmers) and spend their first year of military service on basic training and the last two years farming and defending a border kibbutz. They would provide for security against what were then called Arab infiltrators.

The salonists were no less ready to do their three-year military service, but they looked forward to equipping themselves with professional urban skills. Few followed the highly regarded Prime Minister Ben-Gurion's call to continue the collectivist spirit of transforming the barren land of the Negev in the south.

One significant sign of the changing attitudes that were emerging concerned the Holocaust (Shoah). In the first two or three years after my arrival, I became aware that among many local born Israelis there was a certain disdain for the millions of Jews who allowed themselves to be taken away to be slaughtered without any resistance. The Warsaw Ghetto uprising was much admired, but it was also used to point up the failings of the vast numbers of the others. It was only in 1953, when the Yad Vashem Memorial was built, that attitudes began to change from a lack of respect for the failure of the victims of the holocaust to offer physical resistance to a deeper recognition of their helplessness. However, the major turning point was the 1960 Eichmann trial. Eichman had been the leading Nazi in charge of organizing the murder of the 6 million Jews who were killed in the Holocaust. He had hidden in Argentina, until an Israeli squad assembled explicitly for that purpose captured him. It was his trial which brought home to Israelis and the rest of the world the enormity of what had happened.

Another problem was the gap between the Ashkenazi – mainly East European Jews – and the Sephardi Jews of the Middle East, whose forefathers had been expelled from Spain at the end of the fifteenth century. The former were the socialist founders of the state, and they saw themselves as the bearers of Western modernity. The latter had been largely dispossessed and expelled from the Arab states to arrive in Israel as impoverished refugees. Before their expulsion, many had been culturally and materially relatively well off. Their discriminatory treatment by the Ashkenazi Israeli establishment was much resented. Although the gap between the two communities was bridged in the 2-3 years of compulsory military service, the underlying social and economic disparities were not overcome. The result of the discriminatory treatment was the rise of the outsider Herut Party at the expense of the Mapai Party, which had been the establishment of the new state, and which was now paying the price for discriminating against the Sephardis.

A related problem was that the role and power of the big bureaucracies, which in the smaller versions during the struggles for survival and for independence in the years before the founding of the independent state served the Zionist movement well, had not been adequately prepared as they assumed the responsibilities of governing a population which within a year had doubled in size. For example, the Histadrut, which supposedly represented the workers as their trade union, was also a major employer. Hadar Yoseph had been built by a virtual monopolistic company, which was also in charge of providing amenities for the immigrant inhabitants, including managing the financial arrangements whereby renters would pay the company rent for a certain number of years, after which they could become owners. The local office would be inundated by disgruntled people who sometimes overthrew the tables onto the unfortunate administrators. In addition, the division of responsibilities between the company and the local government was not always clear. On one occasion, for example, my father took both the company and the local government to court to solve an issue involving the discharge of untreated sewage into the disused orange grove nearby.

Finally, a problem which affected our family directly was the civil authority delegated to the Chief Rabbinate. My lack of orthodox credentials as a Jew did not surface in those years. My mother was very much liked and loved by my father's three sisters with whom we were fairly close. Moreover, my mother never really mastered the Hebrew language beyond what was needed for shopping and so on. My father and I were usually on hand to interpret when needed. Hence, she had no difficulty in observing the practice of "don't ask, don't tell". However, the Rabbinate officiated over marriages and death. By international law, Israel was required to recognize marriages that took place abroad, and, as necessary, some couples went to be married in Cyprus to overcome Israel's religious strictures. The Rabbinate also regulated the public observance of the Sabbath – at least as far as public transport was concerned. Buses and trains did not run from sunset on Friday to sunset on Saturday. That allowed taxis to follow the routes of public transport. They reduced their normal charges and were allowed to take on multiple passengers. The Rabbinate also played a part in regulating public education as religious political parties tended to control the government's education portfolio.

Israel's complicated political system always required coalitions of political parties in order to form governments and since the concerns of the religious parties were limited to specific issues of religion and their supporters, they tended to be useful in the formation of coalitions. However, most Israelis are not religiously observant and a social gap was growing between them and those who were highly orthodox. This was particularly true of the Hassidic

Jews. Although they tended to keep themselves to themselves, they did not contribute economically to the country, and, as they gave birth to significantly more children than other Israelis, they were a growing burden on the social services. Another point of contention was that Hassidim were not required to serve in the armed forces.

It is unlikely, that as a fifteen-year old boy I could have clearly articulated and explained what I perceived as underlying problems. But what was and continues to be distinctive about Israel is the openness of the society. There can be few issues and problems that are not discussed and debated – often fiercely and relentlessly. No fifteen-year old would have been unaware of them and especially one who had just been told by his parents that he was to leave the country he had grown to love soon after the end of the summer term at school.

Chapter 3: Encountering My Father's Family

No account of my teenage years in Israel would be complete without reference to the impact on me of the history of my father's family and of the effect it had on my father's generation. The origins of the family go back to Baghdad and beyond that to the Babylonian diaspora and the destruction of the first Temple in Jerusalem more than 2,500 years ago. The notable families, such as Sassoon, Kedouri, Chaim, Ezra, Yahuda (or Judah) and others became major traders in the 17th century, linking Basra in today's Iraq with Bombay (or Mumbai) and Calcutta (Kolkata) with East Asia. The trade became more extensive as the British reached out beyond India in the 18th century. Baghdadi Jews settled in Bombay, Calcutta, and other major Indian cities and ports linking them in the 19th century to Hong Kong, Shanghai, and Kobe. Unlike those of Sassoons, the Yahuda merchants did not deal in opium on religious moral grounds but traded in Indigo and silk. I have a silk Tallit (prayer shawl) that was made for the family in Hong

Kong in 1853. That was the same year in which my branch of the family left for Jerusalem to escape the oppression of the Ottoman rulers and their tax collectors on the eve of the Crimean War.

After arriving in Jerusalem, they established a Yeshiva (a seminary) and bought and farmed land in Motsa, just outside the city. My great grandfather married a lady from a notable family in Vienna, and their beautiful ceremonial wedding bedcover and pillow covers have been passed down to me. They had two sons, my grandfather, Isaac, and his brother, Abraham-Shalom (the 'uncle' of the previous chapter) who were highly distinguished and relatively wealthy. They also had a sister, Sultana, who married one of the Sassoons, whom I only saw once and from a distance. To my knowledge, 'the uncle' had no children, but my grandfather had eight – five daughters and three sons. None of his children reached the distinction of their elders, and, as far as I could make out, the brothers were very conscious of this and in their different ways each sought to make his mark and re-establish past glory.

The brothers (my father and my two uncles) were each talented and intelligent. Their father had ensured that they were well versed in biblical studies. They knew the bible by heart and could identify the chapter and verse of most, if not all, the Hebrew words of the five books of Moses and probably of the prophets and the psalms as well. But as the sons of such an illustrious ancestry, they were anxious to make their own mark in keeping with family traditions. The main problem they confronted was that the world had changed radically since the generation of their elders. Modernity had intruded into the traditional way of life in Jerusalem especially. My grandfather was respected, as what today would be regarded as an old-fashioned patriarch who was guided by established customary behavior – as befitted a learned scion of one of the leaders of

Babylon Jewry in Jerusalem. He participated in public affairs – but within his own frame of reference as a scholar and as a pillar of Jewish orthodoxy. An expert in Islamic law, he was consulted by specialists in the university of Al-Azhar in Cairo, the center of Sunni learning. On one occasion, when the Arabs, led by the Grand Mufti of Jerusalem, instigated rioting in the Old City in 1929, claiming that there was no evidence to show that the so-called 'Wailing Wall' had been the Western Wall of the Jewish Temple destroyed by the Romans, my grandfather published a study tracing irrefutable evidence that it was indeed the Temple Wall. In fact, his study became the basis for a report of the League of Nations on the affair.

However, this same man who had moved the family to the British administered part of Cairo well before World War I to escape the increased taxation levied by the Ottomans, was so observant of Jewish law that he used to make his own wine by boiling raisins at home, lest it be seen by non-Jews, which apparently would have rendered it non-Kosher. There is a story, later confirmed to me by my father's sisters, that when their father, Isaac, returned to Jerusalem bringing with him his youngest daughter and son, who had been born in Cairo, the boy (my father) at the age of 3-4 used to be dressed in the clothes of a girl, when taken outside, so as to avoid the evil eye. The reason for this superstitious behavior may be due to very sad events that underscored the difference between the traditional way of life and the modernity that was beginning to take over. My grandfather had married the love of his life, but she was judged to be 'barren' and her husband felt obliged to divorce her out of honor to his parents. His next wife proved to be fecund, while the first one had to return to the home of her parents, condemned to be ostracized as a social outcast. It was thought that she would be so eaten up inside with bitterness that she could not but feel hatred for the little boy (my father) who was born when his father was fifty years old and the boy

39

was seen therefore as a gift from the Almighty. It was thought that given the opportunity, she would have cast the evil eye over him. From all that I have heard about the rationality and wisdom of my grandfather, he may not have initiated dressing his boy as a girl, but clearly, he did nothing to stop it.

His younger brother, 'the uncle', did not live in Jerusalem and was in many respects very much the modern man. He left for the University of Heidelberg to study under the great German philologist and orientalist, Noerdecke. He was awarded a PhD and, after researching, writing, and teaching in Germany, the Spanish King Alfonso XIII appointed him the first professor of Semitic studies in Madrid. He also became an Egyptologist and claimed some of the practices and rituals carried out by Moses were derived from the Egyptian court. He counted Freud and Einstein among his friends. He was a delegate to the first five Zionist Congresses beginning in Basel in 1897. He acquired a magnificent library of rare Middle Eastern scrolls and manuscripts, as well as incunabula (books published before 1500). Abraham Shalom had bought in auction the religious manuscripts of Isaac Newton, and he had also possessed some of the letters of Napoleon I. In 1951, his library was valued at over $1.5 million dollars (worth more than ten times as much today). Much of the library ended up in the Hebrew University in Jerusalem.

To his deep disappointment, Abraham-Shalom was unable to persuade Weizmann, the Zionist leader, that the founders of Israel should have built on the Jewish legacy of their cultural achievements in Spain (Andalusia), as that would have brought them into cultural interactions with their Arab neighbors. In fact, at the end of his life he wrote a scathing response to Weizmann's autobiography criticizing his refusal to reach out to the Arabs and recognize the culture the two peoples had in common. In recent years there has been a revival of interest in these ideas as younger scholars have begun to research his papers at the Hebrew University in Jerusalem.

Abraham-Shalom was given a state burial in Israel in 1952. His body was shipped to Haifa from Saratoga in the U.S. and, as an eleven-year old, I was privileged to be among the party that accompanied his sarcophagus on the drive to the Jerusalem hills via Tel-Aviv. I remember waving to my school friends, who had the morning-off to witness the motorcade. At the burial place, a large number of people stood a respectful distance from the sarcophagus in the middle of the square they had formed. Suddenly, a little old lady broke away to approach the sarcophagus and lifted the Israeli flag and the rug on its top, gave a little smile and trotted back to her place in the square. I nudged my father to ask who she was and was told, "She's Sultana".

It transpired that Sultana was the sister of 'the uncle' and my grandfather, but I had never heard of her, let alone seen her before. There had obviously been an old schism in the family. Neither my father, nor any of his siblings, went over to pay her their respects. Needless to say, I was not introduced to her, and I never encountered her again.

By this stage, I was becoming familiar with the rifts and divisions in the family, in which my father played an active part. To mark the occasion of our arrival in Israel in the autumn of 1950, the following spring a family Passover gathering was held in the apartment of my aunt, Miriam, in Jerusalem. The apartment had been inherited from my grandfather, and, to my 'English' eyes, it was a throwback to an oriental past. It was in the complex of Makhaneh Yehuda, a large network of buildings with thick walls facing Jaffa Street, the long-standing main road from the old city to Jaffa/Tel-Aviv. It had a large cobblestone courtyard in the middle inside, with a well to provide water to the apartments surrounding it.

Oriental rugs or carpets adorned the walls inside my aunt's apartment, which was furnished in what I took to be the Middle-Eastern style.

The Passover Seder (the ceremonial meal) was led by my father, as the only son of his father who was present. The eldest, Joseph, lived in London and the next oldest, Solomon, lived in Haifa. My three aunts and their husbands also attended. Reina, the eldest, who lived in Tel-Aviv, brought her daughter Ruthie (17) and her son Shraga (15), as well as her husband, Chaim; Hannah and Miriam were childless and lived in Jerusalem. My father began the proceedings with chanting in the Sephardi liturgy, which my mother could not follow, and I could barely do so with my still rudimentary Hebrew, calling on the participants to join in from time to time. Without any forewarning I could see, Reina and Chaim, together with Ruthie and Shraga, suddenly broke away, and at a separate table they carried out the Seder in modern Israeli style, leaving my father and the rest of us to continue with our traditional Sephardi chanting. The evening ended in acrimony.

Later, I found out the background to all this. Hannah and Miriam had greatly disapproved of Reina's marriage in the early 1930s to Chaim, a Hungarian merchant in Tel-Aviv, whom they regarded as uncultured, in addition to not being particularly wealthy. At the time, they made their objections known in no uncertain fashion and the divide between the family in Jerusalem and in Tel-Aviv was never mended. Far from providing an occasion for mending fences, the Seder apparently deepened the divide and not even the arrival of a long 'lost' brother and his family on Passover could overcome the mutual resentment between the two sides. My father kept himself aloof from the underlying contentions, but was clearly unhappy to see his Seder in his father's dwelling disrupted. My mother, who could not follow the proceedings, which were conducted in Hebrew, was nevertheless worried as to what kind of family she had unwittingly joined by coming to Israel. Fortunately, she was very good-natured and was genuinely loved by each of my father's sisters, who all spoke English. In fact, notwithstanding his adherence to traditional customs, my grandfather had taken care to ensure that his daughters, as well as his sons, received a good education. For example, they all spoke several languages and were well read in European literature and Modern Hebrew, in addition to the standard Jewish traditional books for women.

Tolerant and a good mother, Reina was my mother's favorite and not just because she lived relatively nearby in Tel-Aviv. Hannah was more a woman of the world. She had travelled in Europe, paid attention to fashion, and loved the café life Jerusalem had to offer, even though she was what might be called 'streetwise'. In her view, no one got the better of her. Miriam, by contrast, was less interested in the outside world and was a fierce defender of her way of life in Jerusalem. I got on well with each of them. Hannah, in particular, regarded me as the son she never had, but looking back on my relationship with her, I felt a little guarded, as she seemed more concerned with persuading me to adopt her ways and values than being interested in my thoughts and feelings. I got on well with my aunt, Reina, and her husband, Chaim, finding them both warm hearted and well disposed to my mother and me. They had the misfortune to lose their son, Shraga, when he was barely twenty, but their daughter Ruthie who is now in her eighties and has a lovely family with three married daughters, several grandchildren and even great grand-children. Ruthie is the only living member of the Yahuda family with whom I have a close relationship.

Meanwhile an earlier rift in the family involved my uncle Solomon, who lived in Haifa, and my father. The ostensible breaking point was their dispute over the destination of the library of 'the uncle'. As I understand it, there was some confusion over how to interpret his will. In any event it was left to his widow to decide. She came from a wealthy family in South Africa and that was where their marriage had taken place. She decided in the end that her late husband's three nephews, Joseph, Solomon, and my father should be joint trustees to determine the destination of the library, preferably in Israel. Joseph promptly withdrew from the trusteeship, leaving his two brothers to sort matters out. Solomon and my father promptly disagreed: the former wanted to donate it to Bar Ilan University in Tel-Aviv, and my father preferred The Hebrew University in Jerusalem. They were both lawyers and they went to court over the issue. Before the matter could be adjudicated Solomon died, I think from a heart attack, and the library ended up in The Hebrew University.

The division between the two brothers may have been caused, or at least exacerbated by, my father's marriage. Solomon and his wife Naomi, who was the daughter of the Sephardi Chief Rabbi, Yitzhak Nissim, and unlike the other members of the family they were highly observant Jews. Naomi had married the son of the Sephardi Chief Rabbi and she took unkindly to my father having "married out". In any event my mother and I had only seen Solomon and Naomi once and that was on the day we arrived in Haifa on the ship from Marseille back in September 1949. Solomon greeted us at the port and let us stay at his place overnight, before we proceeded to Tel-Aviv. None of us ever spent time with them again.

My aunt Hannah was the only one of the sisters who had ventured out of Israel. She stayed with us in England on at least three occasions. She was always good fun and both my parents and my family with three kids greatly enjoyed her visits. On one occasion, however, she let her 'sophisticated

European mask' slip. She determined that, as a university lecturer in his twenties, I should wear better and more fashionable shoes. She insisted on taking me to a specialty shoe shop in Oxford Street, where after much fuss, she eventually settled on a suitable pair, asked the shop assistant for the price and then made her an offer of 40% less. The flustered young woman had to call the manager. My aunt told him that the price could not be 'fixed'. In her view someone must have arbitrarily chosen the price and she now stood by her offer. After being asked to leave, I tried to explain to her that we were not in a bazaar in Jerusalem and that she had to accept the local practice in London, despite her disapproval. We moved on to a department store in Bond Street and eventually settled on some shoes, without her contesting the price. But she was not happy. Reina was the most highly educated and tolerant of my father's three sisters. She was my mother's favorite.

My encounters with my uncle Joseph, who was thirteen years older than my father, were altogether different. As I'll recount in the next chapter, I had arrived in London in 1956 and didn't know anyone. Although I knew that my father and he had cut off all contact for nearly ten years, I took it upon myself to see if I could mend the rift. At that point, Joseph and his wife, Cecile, lived in Belgravia. Out of the blue I arrived at their door one Sunday. Cecile, a short fat Russian/Ukrainian Jew, didn't know how to deal with me and, greatly flustered, she called out to her husband that his nephew was on the doorstop. She was told to let me in and to send me up a flight of stairs to his study. Without a word of greeting, he immediately drew me into the latest development in the book he was writing, to be entitled Hebrew is Greek. He assured me that it would make him an international wonder. He had worked out a philological matrix that he claimed showed how the Biblical Hebrew writings, and even its grammar, corresponded with those of

Classical Greek, including, where necessary, uses of the ancient dialects of both languages. He was disappointed by my lack of knowledge of Classical Greek, Arabic, and other languages, but he insisted on showing me how he had found the meaning of Biblical words that had eluded traditional commentators and contemporary scholars. He assured me that this book would exceed by far anything accomplished by either his father or his uncle. He said nothing about the break with my father, nor whether my visit had changed that relationship, but I assumed that it had. My father was delighted when I wrote to him about my meeting with Joseph and they soon established close relations, as if nothing had happened to disturb them.

But it transpired that there was more to the relationship than met the eye. My father seemed excessively deferential to Cecile, Joseph's wife, who was a frivolous and not a particularly pleasant woman. Apparently, in the early 1920s my father as a young teenager was sent to stay with his elder brother and his newly married Cecile in Tangiers, because his widowed father found it too taxing to look after the boy. While there, my father developed mumps, and both Joseph and Cecile subsequently blamed him for their inability to conceive children of their own. Whether or not that was the true cause of their infertility, my father seemed to accept responsibility, but he never discussed the issue with me. In any event, I found out at some point in the 1970s, some fifteen years after I had been instrumental in bringing together the two brothers, that Joseph had informed the Sephardic Rabbis at Bevis Marks, the old and revered Synagogue in the City of London, that my mother was not Jewish and as a result neither was I. It was a gratuitously hurtful thing to do. One of the most painful consequences for me was that I was treated as a non-person at my father's funeral, for which I had paid all the expenses out of deference to his wishes to be buried according to the custom of his forefathers.

As I reflect on these encounters, I cannot but help feel sadness and regret for all the discord and bitterness that characterized the relationships within the family. The brothers and sisters of my father's generation, with one or two exceptions, quarreled with each other over all manner of things from the trivial to the important. Each one had admirable qualities and none of them benefitted or profited from all their rows and divisions. Let me give but one example concerning people who loved my mother and me and who were fun to be with and at ease in all societies: my father and his sister Hannah. In the mid 1970s, more than ten years after he had returned to London from Israel, my father asked Hannah to sell his share of the inheritance of the land in Motsa, which she duly did. It was never clear to me why he did not seek the aid of a professional agent. Years later, he came to the conclusion that she had kept back from him some of the money from the sale. The last few years of his life were consumed by a court case in which he accused her in effect of theft and demanded restitution of the money that was allegedly his. He died before the case was settled and, as his only son and heir, I disposed of all the papers and documents and made peace with Hannah.

Underlying all the divisions and rancor, I think, was a generational issue in which none of the brothers and sisters who had grown up in the shadow of the highly distinguished, accomplished and acclaimed father and uncle and surrounded in Jerusalem by other wealthy families from Baghdad, felt that they could measure up to them. Each of the brothers in particular seemed driven by an urge to make his mark on society. They were always treated with honor by the Sephardi Jewish hierarchy in London and in Israel, but that was more out of regard for the standing of the Yahuda family and the

47

accomplishments of their elders. But they seemed to want acclaim for their own distinctions. For example, my uncle Joseph and my father could have had outstanding careers as lawyers. Joseph, in particular, is still remembered in legal circles in London for his use of biblical references and ability to conduct complex cases without reference to written notes. But he devoted himself to research and writing on subjects outside the law that he claimed would change established thought and theories in a fundamental way. For example, he published in 1951 the book New Biology and Medicine and in 1982, Hebrew is Greek. Neither was accepted by specialists in the respective subjects. Similarly, my father sought to become extraordinarily wealthy, and he pursued a variety of schemes, none of which came to fruition. Yet he was highly regarded as a lawyer but did not devote himself to a career in the law.

I think, however, that there was more to the problems of my father's generation than living in the shadow of elders, whose standing and accomplishments exceeded their capacities to reach. The differences between the two generations encompassed the transformation from traditionalism to modernity. My grandfather, especially, was imbued with the learning of the Hebrew and Arabic scholars, rabbis, and judges in lines of continuity going back to Andalusian Spain and beyond. On his own terms, he was prepared to adapt to the new and the modern, ensuring his daughters as well as his sons would be educated to a high level. Yet at the same time, he divorced the woman he loved out of the sense of obligation to his parents and to the injunction of the bible to give birth to children. Moreover, he allowed his little son to be dressed in girl's clothes to defeat the 'evil eye' on the streets of Jerusalem.

By the 1920s, that world was fast disappearing. The Ottoman Empire and its system of government was no more, and the

British Mandate had replaced it in Palestine. By this stage after the end of the First World War, Palestine was being developed at a fast pace. Modern Jewish settlements with a Zionist presence symbolized, perhaps, by the growth of the city of Tel-Aviv beside the ancient city of Jaffa. Apparently, it had been suggested to my grandfather that he might like to invest in the building of Tel-Aviv, but he had refused on the biblical grounds that 'you don't build on sand'. Arguably, 'the uncle', Abraham Shalom, who was not the traditional scholar in the mold of his elder brother, studied in Germany under the great Orientalist and Philologist Noerdecke in Heidelberg, was awarded a PhD, gained the esteem of contemporary European and American scholars and was a friend of notable people. Yet the subjects in which he made his most notable contributions were Judaica and Arabica. In my view, 'the uncle' had a foot in each camp. He was an active Zionist, and his attempts to persuade the Zionist communities of his day to pay more attention to the Jewish culture of Andalusian Spain may have fallen on barren ground in the 1930s, but there are signs of renewed interest in them in the contemporary period, largely the result of access to 'the uncle's papers. They promise to revive a cultural affinity between Arabs and Jews.

Unfortunately, as neither an Arabist nor a Hebraist, I have little or nothing to contribute to the rich theme of cultural accommodation initiated by 'the uncle', but I have benefitted from the extensive and diverse experiences from the encounters with my father's family. Further on in this book I will consider the impact on me and on my intellectual development from the encounters with my mother's New Zealand family. My experiences with my father's family and its antecedents have inculcated in me a profound respect for their cultures and histories, which alone of the ancient minorities in the Middle East have survived into the modern contemporary period. They have done so, not through the enclosed self-referencing world of the East European shtetls, but rather by participating in the world around them. For example, the Jews of 12th Century Spain contributed greatly to the early beginnings of modernity through the cultural interactions with Christians and Moslems. Thus, the great Rabbi Maimonides (The Rambam), who wrote one of the great Jewish classics, *Guide to the Perplexed,* was physician to the famous Moslem leader and fighter Saladin (Salakh-A-Din). To be sure, modern scholarship is a world apart from the modes of scholarship of yesteryear, let alone from that of my forefathers. Nevertheless, my ways of thought and tolerance for other cultures has been greatly enriched by these and related encounters.

Chapter 4: Back to London 1956 – 1966

Despite having spent the first nine years of my life in London, it still seemed a strange place on my return seven years later, on the eve of my sixteenth birthday. Although little had changed in the neighborhood where I had lived before – the houses and streets were much the same – some bombed out areas were now occupied by council houses, and the house where I had lived had been replaced, along with adjoining ones, by modern-looking townhouses. The loss of the flat, the house, its gardens, and surrounds, where I had spent my childhood evoked a strange feeling that an important part of my life had disappeared. My sadness was reflected in the decay of the wider neighborhood. Many of the older, Edwardian upper-middleclass houses had lost their grandeur and become dowdy, especially as not a few had been converted into flats and bed/sitting rooms. People were dressed in old-fashioned clothes, with the predominant color grey, and my overall impression was I had left an open, warm, and optimistic Tel-Aviv to come to a gloomy and dismal London.

Although open discrimination between peoples was less evident in Hampstead, where I lived in various bedsitters, that was not true of other parts of London such as Bayswater, further west, where signs of rooms to rent were accompanied by notices that West-Indians and Irish need not apply. In the seven years I had been away, the demography of London had also changed. In the late 1940s, there was hardly a non-white face to be seen on the streets. By the late 1950s, there were West Indians (who had been recruited to serve on the buses and the underground) and people from South Asia, who came as members of the Commonwealth. London was becoming quite cosmopolitan!

Although I didn't appreciate it at the time, there were signs in the mid-to-late fifties that post-war London was in the midst of a fundamental change – at least as far as the younger generation was concerned. The theater world was shocked by John Osborne's play "Look Back in Anger" and its scorn for the drab deferential middle-class culture of the period. Teenagers accepted with alacrity the defiant, wild beat of rock music from across the Atlantic, as performed by the likes of Bill Haley and the Comets' Rock Around the Clock, which accompanied the anarchical film Blackboard Jungle. The cultural generation divide was epitomized by rock 'n' roll musicians, such as Chuck Berry, Little Richard, Jerry Lee Lewis, Buddy Holly, and, above all, Elvis Presley. There were also local British stars with their own style, including Lonnie Donegan and Cliff Richard. This was the era of the 'Teddy boys', who, when they were not wearing the long jackets associated with the Edwardian period, wore leather jackets and rode motorbikes. They had rivals, known as 'Mods', who wore flashy versions of contemporary middle-class clothes and rode

Vespa-type scooters. Occasionally, the two rival gangs would ride to Brighton for confrontations at the beach.

However, this cultural transformation passed me by, until about two years later, when I encountered it at the local secondary school. Meanwhile, I recovered my enjoyment of irreverent British humor in the surreal anarchy of "The Goons" on the radio or in films, such as The Lavender Hill Mob, The Lady Killers, I'm All Right Jack, etc. In my first four or five years back in London, I spent long periods living by myself. My father was trying to make a career as a lawyer in Israel, leaving my mother to divide her time between her son (me) and my father. She enrolled me at Haverstock Secondary School. It had changed some two or three years earlier from being a secondary modern (i.e., a non-academic school, which did not prepare students for tertiary education) to become a comprehensive school, which supposedly catered equally to students of all abilities. It was, however, conveniently located near the two-bedroom bedsitter we occupied. After a year or so my mother returned to Tel-Aviv to help my father with secretarial work (in English) as he tried to rebuild his legal career. I was left behind to cope on my own as a 17-year old for a year, having been placed in a boarding house not too far away from the school.

Meanwhile, having no friends or other distractions, I focused on my studies. The curriculum was new to me, and my command of English had not advanced much beyond the level of a nine-year old. In those days, Haverstock Hill had not yet had the time to build a reputation as a place of academic achievement. The minimal age at which students could leave school was sixteen, which is what the overwhelming majority of the approximately 1,000 students did. But I was fortunate in the high quality of its dedicated teachers, and in my first year there I exceeded the school record in the number of subjects passed at Ordinary Level (the national examination for students aged 15-16). I was then appointed a "prefect" (a student leader) by the school and went on to be made school captain. I felt strangely detached from the school and did not have the sense of commitment that such a responsible position normally entails. I did, however, feel that I had a duty to uphold the rules of student conduct. Looking back six decades to those years, I realize there was a contradiction between my sense of detachment from the school and my feeling of being duty bound to carry out the responsibilities expected of me by the school authorities. Perhaps the contradiction was a consequence of being left without parental presence and guidance, with the result that I needed to accept some kind of authoritative code of conduct.

One of my responsibilities was to help to maintain order on the playground and during the breaks between classes. That was when I encountered problems with the three gangs in the school, the West Indians (from the Caribbean), the Greek Cypriots, and the local Cockneys. Matters came to a head one day, when after an inconclusive confrontation with the leader of the Cockneys, whose sense of 'honor' I had unknowingly infringed, he demanded we fight each other after school. Being older and bigger, I quickly subdued him without either of us being hurt. Again, he felt humiliated and the following day the older brother turned up with his friends to wait for me almost out of sight beyond the school's fence. A teacher drove me home and the gang picked on two older students, who happened to walk by and beat them up so badly they ended up in hospital. An inflated story was then published in *The Daily Mail* under the headline "Blackboard Jungle Comes to NW3." For the next few weeks, I had to exercise great caution in going about the neighborhood.

While at Haverstock, I had rediscovered my love for cricket and saw the last Test (or international) match of my former hero the great Dennis Compton. In subsequent years, I was able to see the wonderful "Three Ws" of the West Indian team, Worrell, Weekes, and Walcott", as well as their awesome array of fast bowlers. But my real love of sports came from watching English football, or soccer. On my arrival from Israel in the summer of 1956, the only team I had heard of was the Arsenal of north London. I duly went to see their opening game of the season against Cardiff, which ended as a boring nil-nil draw, and even the Arsenal fans booed the team at half time and especially at the end. I was told by one of my neighbors there was another First Division team in north London called Tottenham Hotspur ("The Spurs"). I went to see them the following Saturday and was completely won over, as they beat Leeds United (then one of the stronger teams) 5:1. Since then, I have supported The Spurs through thick and thin for more than 60 years. They have been one of the enduring passions of my life, an experience that has given me insights not only into fandom, but also into how people can become uncritical supporters of performers, causes (political or otherwise), etc., regardless of their success or failure.

In the late 1950s, I often spent evenings at cafés or coffee houses near Swiss Cottage in northwest London, where I met Russian and East European Jews who had a big impact on me. They were different from their equivalents in Israel. Some were former Mensheviks (moderate communists), who fled Lenin's Bolshevik dictatorship; others were former Bundists (socialist Jews), who rejected Zionism. One had even known Trotsky, whom he insisted on calling Lev Davidovitch. They had first escaped to Paris and then, as the Second World War loomed, they came to London, where they settled as émigrés. Others were non-socialists, who had escaped the persecution of both Stalin's Russia and Hitler's Germany to find solace in metropolitan London. Some had rediscovered their-long lost Judaism, but the majority had given up on God. As one explained to me, "never mind the Holocaust, how can one believe in a god who has it in his power to save innocent babies and little children from horrible suffering and terrible deaths and yet does nothing?" A good number of them still retained their adherence to Marxism, and it was these that I engaged most. Quite a few were happy to unburden themselves to me, perhaps because of my having newly come from Israel and my being able to answer some of their queries about the Jewish state. They certainly gave me much to think about, and they enlarged my view of the world. They enabled me to understand something of the Marxist viewpoint and of the nature of the arguments and the divisions between them. By observing and thinking about them I gained insights into the complexities and underlying sadness of the lives of emigres. Many years later, these encounters helped me to understand better the factionalism to which Chinese political exiles were prey.

Before the end of my school year in the summer of 1959, I had to choose a subject I wished to study and the university at which to pursue that course of study. My main academic interest was history, but I felt at a disadvantage to other English students, whom I assumed would have been immersed in British and European history over a good number of years. At my advanced history course at school, I had studied the medieval period in Europe and had become fascinated with the emergence of modernity, which I took to have been sparked by the interplay between Moslem, Jewish, and Christian cultures and religions in the 12th-13th centuries in the Mediterranean, centered on Spain. At that time, I could find no such undergraduate course at any British University. Nor could any of the teachers at Haverstock give me any advice, as their experience of finding university places for their students was limited. Indeed, they were taken aback by my having applied to colleges in Cambridge and Oxford, which they saw as being too ambitious. But as it turned out, the responses from Oxbridge were favorable, and I was told I could be accepted to courses in Middle Eastern studies, which I then had the temerity, in the view of my teachers, to turn down. However, by then I had some experience of British views of developments in the Middle East, especially in the light of Britain's Suez misadventure. My views were formed by the perspectives from Israel, where the feeling was that the army had retaliated successfully against Egyptian military threats and the promotion of infiltrators, only to be let down by the failings of the British, the French, and the Eisenhower administration. In retrospect, perhaps I should have seen the episode as the key turning point of the end of the British empire and its great power pretensions. In any event, I found British attitudes toward Israel condescending and over critical.

My interest in the historical sources of modernity took me further east to China. I could have chosen India, which as a democracy with English as its official language, would have been much more accessible for me. But I was put off by what I took to be the general disdain for India and its cultures, as demonstrated, for example, by the small space allocated at that time to Indian artefacts in the British Museum in comparison to the expansive rooms allowed to those from China or Japan. In addition, I had become aware of what was later called the 'Joseph Needham question' (the principal author of the multiple-volume *Science and Civilization in China*), as to why traditional China did not embark upon industrialization. By the 11ᵗʰ century China and its neighboring peoples had invented what the British philosopher Francis Bacon (1561-1626), often regarded as the founder of the scientific method, called the four inventions on which the modern world was built: namely, paper, printing, the magnetic compass, and gunpowder.

However, Bacon did not know the provenance of all four was from China. From Needham's perspective, China had the other prerequisites, including flourishing domestic and external trade systems, extensive concentrations of capital for investment, a well-organized state, and unsurpassed skill in managing the flows and damming of major rivers. The Sociologist Max Weber, who is famous for identifying the emergence of Protestantism as the necessary condition for the rise of capitalism in the West, had argued that the failure of traditional China to modernize was due to its Confucian system. Ironically, in the late 20th century, it was argued by the Singaporean leader Lee Kuan Yew and others that it was precisely the Confucian legacy of its values and practices that enabled the East Asian Sinitic sphere to modernize and industrialize so rapidly and successfully. If Weber faulted Confucianism for deemphasizing individualism in favor of communalism and the bureaucratic state it had fostered, it was precisely the social discipline associated with Confucianism that Lee extolled. However, neither explained the provenance in China for the path-breaking discoveries Bacon regarded as the foundation pillars on which modernity was built.

In order to study these issues in sufficient depth, I determined I should acquire knowledge of Chinese language and culture. To this end, I sought admission to the School of Oriental and African Studies of the University of London, and much to my surprise, was admitted after a brief interview with one of the lecturers to the course "Modern Chinese Language and Literature". Unfortunately, I found I was no linguist, but I could reach a level acceptable to first year examiners by dint of hard study and through memorizing Chinese characters written on one side of small cards with the meaning and pronunciation on the other side. I had literally hundreds of such cards, which I would seek to etch in my memory through repeated study at every opportunity, such as in the course of travel, or whenever

I had free time. My pronunciation was fine, but at no point could I hold a proper conversation in Chinese. At that time, China was closed to foreign visitors and the Chinese spoken in London's small Chinatown was Cantonese and Hokien – not Mandarin, which I was studying. What is more, unlike many experts, admirers, and aficionados of China and things Chinese, I did not much care for Chinese poetry and painting. For one thing, Classical Chinese was beyond my comprehension and for another, much of the poetry in translation (even by such a master as Arthur Waley) seemed to evoke the same imagery and themes in poems written by scholars as they took leave from their friends at the gates of Beijing en route to an appointment in the provinces.

At no point could my teachers and professors be blamed for what some would have regarded as my 'Philistine attitudes'. I was taught by scholars, some of whom were already, or went on to become, some of the most illustrious names in Sinology. These included experts on Chinese fiction from the 12th to the 18th centuries, such as Patrick Hannan and Cyril Birch; experts on Chinese ancient philosophy, such as Angus Graham and D.C. Lau; and historians, such as Dennis Twichett and Michael Loewe. I learned much from each of them. In particular, I remember the insights of D.C. Lau into the linguistic reasons for the absence of abstract concepts in the writings of early Chinese philosophers, such as was evident in the writings of their ancient Greek contemporaries around the 5th century BCE. The grammar of classical Greek enabled a writer to identify a word precisely according to whether it was, say, a noun, an adjective, or a verb. Moreover, the use of a verb could be further narrowed as to whether it was transitive or not and in what tense it was being applied. The sentence in which these categories of speech were used could be subject to further distinctions. None of this applied to classical Chinese, where a single word (i.e., character) could be used in all these ways.

For example, the word for 'King' (Wang) was used by Confucius without change of word (i.e., written character) to stand for being a king, a good king, or for ruling in a kingly way.

In Classical Chinese, philosophers often had no alternative but to express abstract concepts in elusive and illustrative ways. A famous example is "White horse not a horse" (Baima feima ye), which in plain English translation means that a white horse is just one form of a horse, and it cannot be representative of the quality of all horses. In other words, this was a Chinese version of concept of the Platonic ideal. Another example is the rejection of what we came to know as 'positivism' (associated with Auguste Comte – the 18ᵗʰ century philosopher), in a saying attributed to the philosopher Zhuangze of the 4ᵗʰ century BCE, who claimed he didn't know whether he was a grasshopper pretending to be a philosopher, or a philosopher pretending to be a grasshopper. In other words, things may be the opposite of what they seem. However, one of the abiding lessons I learned from my partial studies of Chinese philosophers was that the absence of a belief in an almighty god was no barrier to the development of high levels of ethics, of no lesser value than those of the Abrahamic religions of Judaism, Christianity, and Islam. Moreover, the Chinese were by and large spared the horrendous religious wars and schisms which darkened the histories of Europe and the Middle East. As I was to suggest to students in later years, studying China and its ways was enormously helpful in understanding one's own society and culture. It served to counteract the instinctive view that the beliefs and practices of one's own society constituted the norm, against those of other societies which deviated from that norm.

Classical Chinese with its complex allusions and subtleties was linguistically beyond me, but I was fascinated by the concepts underlying traditional concepts of nature which included both a reverence for the forces of nature, such as the many facets of water, and the practical approach, as seen in the development of means to harnessing water to serve human needs. The ambiguities displayed with regard to water, for example, went to the heart of the development of Chinese civilization as we know it. In the world of nature espoused by Daoism (or Taoism), water was esteemed for its unique character of being soft enough to immerse your hand in it, of being colorless, and of always seeking to be level and placid – yet it always sought to move from high ground towards the sea, and once roused, it could penetrate anything and nothing – not even rocks – could withstand its progress. Confucians, on the other hand, saw rivers as waters to be trained and regulated to serve the needs of agriculture and to play an indispensable part in the building of the Chinese state and empire. As I matured with age and intellect, I came to see the importance of how the continuing encounter with China's traditional civilization contributed to my appreciation of the great diversity inherent in human societies, none of which could claim to be the exclusive exemplars of virtue and best practice.

Fortunately, modern Chinese – and especially contemporary China – was more accessible to me. I became fascinated by the debates of Chinese intellectuals in the early years of the 20th century, about the best way to modernize their country after the collapse of the last dynasty amid the perceived failings of the Confucian social order. Not only could I actually read their writings in the original Chinese, but the debates themselves were fascinating, especially between those who advocated the path of Western pragmatism and democracy and those who favored anarchism or who sought to follow the example of the Russian revolution.

Meanwhile I became entrapped by the game of Go (Wei Qi in Chinese). A Japanese master (4ᵗʰ Dan -amateur) visited SOAS and took pleasure in teaching three of us in the student common room by playing games with each of us in turn when he had the time. He left at the end of my second year and, fortunately for me SOAS decided to make the Chinese course a four-year degree and I was able to reach a high enough standard to be eligible to move towards studying for a PhD.

By this point in 1963, I was married with two children, Tamar (Tammy) and Daniella. The third, David, was born in 1965. My wife had been a fellow student at Haverstock, who had been a year ahead of me and had left for university, but she withdrew before completing her first year. We met again in 1960 and she became pregnant, leading to our marriage in May 1961 and the birth of our first daughter in December. The two other children soon followed. At the time, a brief window of opportunity opened up to recent graduates of Chinese studies in the UK to go to China as assistant teachers of English. A few of my fellow graduates seized the rare opportunity to live in China for two years. Doubtless had I still been single, I too would have gone there. On reflection, however, I am not persuaded the experience of those who went was entirely beneficial. To be sure, they returned with excellent spoken and written Chinese, but in their different ways they had been unduly influenced by their Chinese experiences and found it hard to maintain their own independent perspectives.

In any event, I stayed in London and received a fellowship enabling me to transfer to the Department of Economic and Political Studies at SOAS, where I was registered to pursue a research degree on rural political control in China. The research took much longer than anticipated, in part because at that time in 1964-65 my supervisors were not specialists in Chinese politics and in part because there was much about developments in Chinese agriculture that were hidden from view. It was only in 1966 that SOAS appointed a professor in Chinese politics (Dr. Stuart Schram). By this time the pressure of being a research student and caring for a family of a wife and three young children had become too great.

On the advice of an older graduate student, I decided to sit for a Master's examination, which would enable me to get a paid job. I had to register with the University in three days, before the end of March 1966, in order to be able sit for the examination in June. I had two supervisors, one a specialist on the economics of Chinese agriculture and the other, a political scientist with an interest in the politics of the Middle East. The form had to be signed by both supervisors. The first to arrive the following morning was the economist who duly signed. On seeing that signature, the other professor refused to sign on the grounds that by having the economist sign I indicated that I wanted to be an economist. On appealing to the SOAS registrar, she noted more in sorrow than in anger, "those two are not at it again?" She advised to get a new form and tell the Politics professor that you had seen the error of your ways and once he signed, I was to go to the economist and tell him about the other professor and she was sure that all would be well. And that was how the matter was resolved. But the affair gave me an insight into the malevolent consequences of academic infighting. My respect for the two academics, who were highly accomplished in their fields of study, was further diminished when I found neither was able to give me a syllabus to give to the university authorities, and they told me to write one. Before the end of the day I got approval for what I had written, which was as comprehensive as I could make it. I could not afford to have it rejected. Fortunately, a thesis was not required, and the university regulations allowed instead for a three-hour essay to be written under examination conditions. Two days later, after all the formalities were over, I began to prepare for the

Master's examination in June in the Government and Politics of China.

Happily, I not only passed, but passed with 'distinction'. Even more significant for me was that the external examiner was Professor Joseph Frankel, the founder and head of the Department of Politics at the University of Southampton. He had previously been at the University of Aberdeen where he had met my supervisor, the economist, who had chosen him to be my external examiner. Frankel liked my examination script, especially my 3 hour-essay on Mao Zedong, and invited me to apply to a lectureship in his department. Fortunately, I did well in the interview and was appointed more or less right away. That began a new chapter in my life. Frankel had studied philosophy in Poland, before leaving for Australia. After the Second World War, he joined the University of Aberdeen in Scotland and in 1960 founded the Department of Politics at Southampton University. By this time, he had gained a reputation in political theory and as an early writer on the making of foreign policy, but he was also highly knowledgeable about the politics of the Soviet Union and the Soviet Bloc. I was fortunate to have such a rich cultured and learned person as my first head of department.

As I look back on the ten years since my arrival in the UK from Israel, I can see my life and my outlook on life had changed immeasurably. For one thing, by the age of 25 I was married and had three children. That was too early an age to take on such responsibilities, especially as I had pursued academic studies. In 1966, it was still possible to gain academic employment without a research degree, but that door to the academic profession soon closed and the qualification of a PhD became a necessary requirement. Perhaps that was inevitable, because of the greater emphasis on professionalism in all walks of life, but I can think of many older distinguished university scholars who contributed much to the development of their subject, and who were inspirations to their students, who did not even have a Master's degree. Among those whom I knew, Alec Nove (1915-1994) was perhaps the most highly regarded expert on the economy of the Soviet Union of his day. Some of the greatest and most influential scholars in my discipline of International Relations had only Bachelor degrees. To name but two whom I knew as friends and colleagues, Hedley Bull (1932-1985) and Susan Strange (1923-1998) who are still regarded as leaders of theories of the 'English School' and 'International Political Economy' respectively. I would not claim to be similarly distinguished, but I refer to them as indicating that 'training towards obtaining a PhD', in what has become the sine qua non for budding academics in the United States and in the UK from the 1970s onwards, was not the case when I was first appointed in 1966. Nor do I think I have been disadvantaged by not having completed a PhD thesis, especially as I have successfully supervised many PhD research students.

But to return to my reflections on that decade of my return to the UK, I had gained in self-reliance and self-confidence. My experiences had opened new worlds for me, and I had gained deeper understanding of different cultures and ways of thought. As the move to London in 1956 was abrupt, especially after I had established friendships and had begun to set down roots in Israel, it was difficult to develop new friends in England, and since my focus was on studying, I became more introverted. I also became more ill-at-ease in society and found socializing difficult. It had the effect of accentuating my sense of being different from others, of being something of an outsider. Having been cut-off from what I consider normal family life, I think in retrospect I missed the love and advice of parents as I emerged into adulthood.

On the positive side of my experience of the decade, I learned to look at the experiences of other people with an unusual degree of empathy, perhaps because I was not rooted in a particular group and was sufficiently detached so as to feel the need to avoid antagonistic relationships and to mitigate potential conflict. Because I had moved three times abruptly at a relatively young age between two countries, I had become adaptable, but it was often painful to lose the camaraderie of friendships, and it was not easy to start all over again in new countries. Despite often feeling lonely, I had to get on with different kinds of people in different places, and I developed a degree of detachment in the ways I related to people and their diverse cultures. I became more of an observer than an active participant, and I became more abstractly analytical in describing and thinking about events, people, and their relationships. By standing back, rather than being directly involved, I became more understanding of peoples and cultures different from my own, but that also enhanced a sense of relative isolation.

Even though the country never lost its hues of grey in my eyes, there was much about England to admire in those days. By the end of the 1950s, a new youth culture was emerging that was to blossom in the carefree 1960s. Britain was shedding its colonial empire at an ever-faster pace, just as it was accepting more migrants from what was now called the 'Commonwealth'. The signs of rooms to rent in parts of London, which said the West Indians and Irish need not apply, had disappeared. Although there was evidence of social tension, London, at any rate, had become a more tolerant city, in which people from all parts of the world were accepted, though not always welcomed.

My sense of myself as a cosmopolitan was enriched by my studies of Chinese history and politics. The diversity of its culture and indeed the characteristics of its orthodox or mainstream culture and history were unfamiliar to most of my English contemporaries. In the mid 1960s, before the West had embraced China's opening to the world in the early 1970s, China – and its culture – was relatively unknown. Even those regarded as among the most cultured and highly educated in Europe and the United States would not have been able to identify by name a single Chinese writer of the last 1,000 years, yet they would have been expected to be familiar with the great Russian writers and with the outlines of Islam. No wonder I felt unusually enriched intellectually, but at the same time somewhat outside the mainstream. There were few people with whom I could discuss some of the main themes that were of interest to me, such as comparisons between Soviet and Chinese communism. Fortunately, one such person was my new professor, Joseph Frankel.

Chapter 5: Southampton 1966-1972

My stay at Southampton University for six years was notable for shaping my academic career as a specialist on China's foreign policy, with an interest more broadly in Southeast Asia. The latter arose from lecturing and discussing aspects of the Vietnam War with officers from the UK Southern Command, which had a mutually beneficial relationship with the University's Department of Politics. As I shall explain later, it was through the auspices of Southern Command that I was able to visit Hong Kong for six weeks in 1968, which was my first visit to East Asia.

My lectureship at Southampton also broadened my experience and understanding of politics and international politics, which has stood me in good stead ever since. I am also grateful to my colleagues from the Department of Politics for welcoming me warmly as a participant in their academic endeavors and for being unstinting in their advice in enabling me to become more proficient in combining political theory with pragmatic analysis.

However, it was with relief and a measure of apprehension that I began my lectureship at the University of Southampton. At the age of 25, married with three children, I was finally in a position to provide for the family and begin a career as an academic. All my struggles to reach the appropriate grades in the ten years of studying various subjects since leaving Israel had not been in vain. Nevertheless, I realized that formidable challenges lay ahead in both my personal and academic lives, but I also felt my sets of experiences had given me an independence of outlook and an inner self-confidence I felt would see me through.

Perhaps the most difficult of the problems facing me was saving my faltering marriage. On reflection, I started a family when I was far too young, especially when my wife and I lacked the independent financial means to support ourselves. My parents and my mother in law did their best to help us, but they too were struggling, especially in the early years of our marriage. But even as we began to recover financially, we found we were growing apart. As I look back on my early marriage and on the birth of three children, before I could really afford to look after them financially and before I was properly mature, that doubtless put too heavy a strain on the marriage. Not surprisingly, the marriage came to an end, and my wife and I were divorced in 1972. Despite that, I really enjoyed the early years with my children. The divorce, however, effectively brought my stay in Southampton to an end.

Fortunately, the strain of a gradual and often painful breakdown of the marriage did not prevent me from making progress in my academic work. Strangely, my academic work may have benefited, as a mechanism for detaching me from my marital problems. Reading, teaching, researching, and writing required particular focus and concentration, which could only be achieved by a detachment from other matters. My earlier life of mobility and change had made me less engaged with others. I had become more aloof socially, more self-reliant, and content with my own company. This did not mean I did not appreciate and enjoy the company of others, but it resulted in my becoming less dependent on the social support of others. In any event, I was able to meet the requirements of my obligations as an academic.

The main academic challenge I faced was not being technically well prepared for the teaching I was obliged to undertake. The Politics Department I had joined sought to ease my entry into its teaching program by allocating me a class to run on British politics 101. This was the main first year course in which one of the senior members of the department would deliver an introductory lecture series for all the students who would then be divided into groups of about fifteen each for the purpose of presenting essays on and discussions of the topics of the lectures. Ordinarily, taking such a class would ease the entry of a new teacher, but my problem was I had never taken a course in British politics and my background in the study of politics had been confined to a one-year course in American politics and several years of my own study of Chinese politics. Consequently, I immersed myself in the study of the topics for the classes in the two to three months before the start of the term. Not surprisingly, I over prepared and I very quickly noticed I was not getting the full attention of the students. I then changed tack and initiated discussions on broader issues such as, what is 'politics,' and what is the role of a legislature, as opposed to technicalities of the workings of parliament.

I also found I could not expect the university library to acquire the range of books and journals needed in order to set-up a special course on the politics of China as an option for third year students. The Politics Department budget for library acquisitions was necessarily limited and had to serve the needs of all the dozen or so other members of the department. Although I didn't appreciate it at the time, I came to understand why the other professor in the department, whose special interest was in British local- government, told me he thought my appointment was "exotic". As my second year loomed, I was encouraged to take over Professor Frankel's course on Soviet politics, which was seemingly related to the politics of the other major communist party state – China. Frankel would also be freed to pursue other studies of more immediate interest to him. I readily agreed, even though it required me to embark on yet a new course of study. In fact, I found the best way to learn a subject was to teach it. Arguably, an outsider such as myself, who was more familiar with the Chinese (Maoist) communist approaches, could bring fresh comparative insights into the study of Soviet politics. But that is not for me to say and it is something better left to my students to observe. I did feel intellectually enriched by being in a position to compare the one with the other.

My Visit to Hong Kong in 1968

The Politics Department had a special program on 'Defense Studies', which gave it an institutional link to the Southern Command of the British armed forces, prior to its merger with the UK Land Forces in 1972. In other words, the association with the Politics Department lasted through to the end of my stay at the university. During that period, I was called upon to give occasional lectures on the Vietnam War, the Cultural Revolution, Sino-Soviet relations, and the beginnings of the Sino-American rapprochement. As a result, I had to become familiar with a whole new range of academic issues underlying pressing practical questions, such as the problems in the conduct of the Vietnam War, or how best to explain the deepening divide between the two great communist powers. I found myself drawn more and more into questions fundamental to the academic discipline of International Relations. In fact, my first published academic articles sought to explain changes in Chinese foreign and strategic policies.

Lecturing to military offices required a different approach from teaching students or presenting academic papers. Officers responded best to crisp point by point presentations to which they could relate their experiences and to which they could contribute and raise questions. Although Britain did not actively participate in the American war in Vietnam, British troops had been the first Western forces to take the surrender from the Japanese occupiers of Vietnam and to prepare the way for the return of the French colonial forces, who then contested with Ho Chi Minh and his Vietminh for control initially of the north of the country. In that context, I had occasion in the late 1960s to meet a British officer who claimed to have briefly detained Ho Chi Minh in 1945 or 1946. He said he then released Ho under pressure from his HQ.

It was thanks to my association with Southern Command I was able to visit East Asia for the first time. Professor Frankel interceded on my behalf, and I was able to join a British military passenger flight to Hong Kong from Brize-Norton in Oxfordshire. I was given the nominal rank of Lieutenant Colonel, and I soon found out why it was necessary, as the plane stopped at each of the major bases of the old empire, beginning in Malta. The passengers included military families, regular servicemen, sergeants, and officers, and at each stop the men of the different ranks would go straight to their respective bars (or 'messes'), drink a good deal, totter back to their seats on the plane, and sleep until the next stop. As an ostensibly senior officer, I automatically had access to the officers' mess. After Malta, the plane stopped at bases in Cyprus, Bahrain, The Maldives, Diego Garcia, Singapore, and, finally, Hong Kong. Not long after leaving the UK, I developed a raging toothache in one of my back molars and welcomed the drinks on offer, even though they did not induce any sleep.

On arrival in Hong Kong late at night, the military and their families were met and whisked off to their destinations. But I trundled off alone, away from the military section of the Kai-Tak airport, and walked into adjacent Kowloon, with the aim of finding a hotel room for the night. It was past midnight and, to my amazement, the streets were full of life with hustle and bustle and with illuminations in Chinese and English casting light everywhere. Young kids were still helping their parents prepare food for their street stalls. The tropical heat only added to the unfamiliar smells and an atmosphere and a way of life I had never encountered before. Not even my overwhelming toothache, lack of sleep, and jetlag detracted from the scene which engulfed my senses. But I needed a room for the night, with what seemed little time to spare, so I eventually collapsed into a clean looking Irish-named hotel. The following morning, I made my way to the Universities Service Center, which catered to Western scholars with research interests in China. It will be recalled that such Westerners were denied access to the People's Republic of China in the 1960s. The Center's director, who was an imposing Chinese gentleman dressed in a formal suit, received me, a bedraggled looking westerner claiming to be a scholar, with a degree of disdain, bordering on disbelief. I was accepted only after one of the resident scholars recognized and vouched for me.

While waiting, I cast my eye at the local newspaper, whose front page was taken over by reports and photographs of Chinese corpses with their hands still bound at the back in barbed wire, who had washed up on the outer beaches of Hong Kong. Apparently, they were the victims of factional fighting in the Cultural Revolution in southern China and had been tossed into the Pearl River, to float down the estuary to Hong Kong. It was a harsh introduction to the realities of Chinese political life just across the border. Vivid memories of the photos of the decomposing corpses have remained in my mind ever since, and, although I have rarely had occasion to refer to them, they have played a part in my thinking about some of the characteristics of Chinese politics ever since.

I spent six weeks of the summer of 1968 in Hong Kong. I became acquainted with a number of American graduate research students, some of whom went on to become well known and accomplished scholars. I visited bars and encountered American sailors and soldiers on Rest and Reaction from the Vietnam War and got to know some of their bar girls. One of them once gave me an insight into Chinese nationalism or racism, despite the country's low prestige at that time: "Once there was a master baker and in baking his first loaves of bread, he was anxious to retrieve them from the oven. They turned out to be white and under-baked – all the white people in the world. He let the second set of loaves stay in the oven too long. The result was that they were black and over-baked – the black people. But his third set were baked a delicious golden yellow – all the Chinese people in the world." Clearly racism was not just the prerogative of colonialists and white people!

The local academics from Hong Kong and Taiwan, whom I got to know thanks to the broad range of people attracted to the Universities Service Center, had a distinctive way of thinking about Chinese and indeed regional politics. Their emphasis was on individual political leaders and their various personalist links and associations, rather than on the more abstract theorizing that characterized much of Western scholarship about politics in East Asia. In so far as these Asian scholars thought about theory, they did so within the context of Realism, understood as the significance of power and interest politics. The late Roderick MacFarquhar, the leading Western specialist on the politics of China's Cultural Revolution, once characterized the subject of his study as "Mao against the rest." That title would have won instant acceptance in East Asia, but he thought that it would not be taken seriously in the West, so he refrained from using it. That emphasis on the personal characteristics of leaders necessarily led to much gossip and speculation, but underlying that were distinct understandings about the nature of political authority and the attendant political culture from which that authority emerged. I did not immediately absorb these insights or grasp their explanatory power at the time, but my six weeks' stay in Hong Kong, brief though it was, alerted me to important differences between my thinking about politics and authority that was derived from Western historical experience and theorizing and that which I had come across in metropolitan Hong Kong.

The Ructions of the Late 1960s

The students at Southampton were inspired and affected by the student movements elsewhere in the West. They were not in virulent conflict with university authorities for their supposed endorsement of the Vietnam War, nor did they spark upheavals in the streets, as their Parisian counterparts did. They did not even lead huge demonstrations, as their London associates did. By comparison, Southampton was somewhat off the beaten track for journalists and television producers, yet students did organize protests and occasional disruptions within the university and helped to change forever the sense of deference towards authority. They brought the cultural changes to Southampton associated with the generational change in which the young broke through the social restrictions of the post-world war habits and style to display a more open and hedonistic way of life.

International events seemed to support and promote these new trends and the promise of a different future they portended. The impact of the Tet Offensive in Vietnam brought to an end the presidency of Lyndon Johnson and caused the two presidential candidates, Nixon and McGovern, to base their electoral campaigns on the promise to end the war. The 1968 Spring Uprising in Czechoslovakia suggested that even the Communist Bloc was about to undergo far-reaching reforms, which would lead to greater freedom. Some people chose to see the Chinese Red Guards as harbingers of a common future for the radical young across the world. But by the end of the year, these hopes for radical change had been thoroughly disappointed. The Czech uprising had been crushed by Russian tanks, Nixon's electoral victory did not lead to the end of the War, but to its intensification under the guise of 'peace with honor', at least to start with. The Red Guards had taken up vicious factional fighting and were dispatched to the countryside to 'learn from the peasants'.

Much as I had sympathized with the aspirations of the students of 1968, I did not set much store by them. Their goals were ill thought out and, as far as the politics of the movements were concerned, they antagonized those, such as organized labor, whose support or even neutrality would have been useful. Internationally, the new president, Nixon, was hardly in favor of changes sought by students, and his approach to ending the Vietnam War did not concur with theirs. I was not surprised by the general counter reaction that set in, bringing to an end the high hopes and cultural excesses in the West of 1968.

By this stage, I found myself called upon from time to time by the BBC World Service programs to answer queries about developments in China and in the Vietnam War. In particular the BBC seemed to be interested in the aims and outlook of the protagonists and their chances of success. This was a new departure for me, which fortunately did not challenge me unduly, except that in the absence of reliable information on say political developments behind the scenes in China, I had to resort to explaining why the official view was misleading and then try to make sense of developments in China within a broader perspective. But given that so much about China was especially obscure and unknown in the late 1960s, I was able to utilize my background knowledge to good effect.

The military crushing of the Czech Spring occasioned the so-called 'Brezhnev Doctrine', by which the Soviet Union arrogated to itself the right to intervene militarily in any communist country whose socialist system was deemed to be in danger of being overthrown. In the context of the deterioration of Sino-Soviet relations, Moscow began to send large military forces to the vicinity of China. Actual conflict between the two giant countries took place first in March 1969, when the Chinese ambushed a Soviet patrol on a disputed island in the Ussuri River in the Far East. The incident led to further skirmishes, until the Soviet military using their more advanced conventional armored forces made an incursion deep into Xinjiang (the region containing China's nuclear weapons) in the summer. Although that led to an undeclared cease-fire, the Soviet leaders apparently considered destroying the Chinese military nuclear facilities, but they first sought to sound out the likely Western reaction. Their diplomats contacted what they regarded as influential academics, as well as various government agencies in the West. One even came to Southampton in the autumn of that year to seek my views, despite my relatively low status. Perhaps I was contacted because I had written a couple of academic articles on China as a nuclear power and had made a few broadcasts on related subjects. In any event, it was not until the CIA disclosed the enquiries made by Soviet diplomats that Nixon and Mao took the immediacy of the Soviet threat seriously, which then sparked-off their search for a Sino-American alignment.

I spent the academic year October 1969 - June 1970 as a fellow at the Institute for International Studies at the London School of Economics, where I shared a room with John Gittings, who was on leave from *The Guardian* Newspaper. His views were to the left of mine, but he enjoyed an international reputation as a China scholar, and we shared an interest in analyzing the exciting changes taking place in Sino-American relations in the context of their respective relations with the Soviet Union and in the ending of the Vietnam War. He was also in the process of completing his book, *The World and China 1922-1972*, and I was working on what appeared to be differences among the Chinese elite about relations with the Soviet Union on the eve of the Cultural Revolution; that became the controversial article, "Kremlinology and the Chinese Strategic Debate, 1965-1966", published in *The China Quarterly*, (January 1972) the leading academic journal on Chinese studies at the time. The main benefit for me, however, arose from the opportunity to exchange views with John Gittings about the fast-changing developments then taking place in Chinese politics, and how they related to relations with the great powers, the ending of the Vietnam War, and to Korea. He had been studying and writing about these matters in depth for several years. It was the first time for me to be able to discuss topics of my primary scholarly interests with a scholar of repute.

Initially, I was influenced by Gitting's leftist approach. Doubtless the cynicism with which the Nixon-Kissinger leadership carried out the bombing campaign in Cambodia – supposedly to compel the North Vietnamese to negotiate, coupled with the support they gave to the West Pakistan army in its vicious campaign against the Bengali people of West Pakistan, in order to demonstrate strategic support for China – eased the way for me to take a more hostile view of the American administration, however, the ideological rigidities underlying the leftist viewpoints brought my leftist flirtation to an end. I found the quasi-Marxist emphasis on class struggle and on historical determinism unsatisfactory, especially as it downplayed the significance of human agency in favor of abstract forces. Like most social and political theories, the Marxist variants tended to focus on particular aspects of highly complex social interactions.

A German Interlude

On my return to Southampton in the summer of 1970 after the year's leave, I participated in the exchange agreement the Department of Politics had with its equivalent in Goethe University, near Frankfurt Am Main in the wine-growing region of West Germany. It was a thoroughly enjoyable experience, relaxing with agreeable colleagues, drinking newly produced white wine, as we discussed Anglo-German differences in systems of education, the organization of industry, and the character of socialism.

I was struck by the superior technical and maths education on offer in Germany. For example, even in a relatively small town the quality and variety of geometrical precision instruments in the local store available for sale put to shame what was on display in supposedly similar stores in London. On a visit to Tokyo about ten years later, I had a similar experience. That gave me insight into why both German and Japanese manufacturers enjoyed such a high reputation for the quality of their engineering and their finished products. I came to understand something about the advantages of what has been called the "familism" or "paternalism" of some large German and Japanese firms. The German practice of having workers representatives on company boards, apparently contributed to a sense of community between management and labor and the avoidance of the kind of antagonistic class struggle, characteristic of much of British industrial relations. The German and Japanese sense of community in places of work doubtless contributed to the pride producers took in the quality of their work.

Leaving Southampton

What finally brought my marriage to an end was the departure of my wife with a colleague in the department, effectively leaving the three children in my care. I decided to leave the town and the university and, if possible, move to London. I wanted to make a clean break from the place where I had experienced much sadness and not a little trauma, even though my academic career had prospered. I did not want to encounter the inevitable emotional difficulties in renewing relationships with local friends and colleagues. Besides which, London could offer academic opportunities where I would no longer be treated as "exotic", or where I would be asked to explain why I had chosen to specialize in Chinese studies.

I had benefited greatly from my seven years at Southampton University. I had learned much about teaching at a number of different levels to a variety of audiences, and I knew how to organize academic courses. I had researched and published articles in both specialized and more general journals in the UK and the USA. Opportunities had arisen to exchange academic views with scholars in Germany and in Hong Kong, where I been able to gain some experience of East Asia at a critical time in China's Cultural Revolution. Above all, Southampton had extended my intellectual horizons in a friendly, but challenging environment.

As it happens, in the summer of 1972, the prestigious London School of Economics and Political Science (LSE) advertised for a lectureship in International Relations (IR). I applied, despite not having been tutored in IR and being unfamiliar with the arguments involving the different schools of thought central to the discipline. I immersed myself in one of the introductory books on the subject, but I was fortunate in the timing of my interview at the LSE in the autumn, which took place in the aftermath of the complex rapprochement between China and the US engineered by Mao Zedong and Zhou Enlai on the one side and Richard Nixon and Henry Kissinger on the other. Most of the interview was devoted to that subject, about which I knew more than the interviewers. To be fair, I was also asked about IR as an intellectual discipline, but perhaps luckily for me, there was not sufficient time to explore that in depth. Thus, I began my appointment at the LSE in 1973.

Chapter 6: Return to London 1973

The return to London as a university teacher at the LSE transformed my life. It was more than a 'homecoming'. It was an embarkation on a new way of life, in which I came to be regarded as distinctive rather than exotic. There were others in my IR department who had special interests in far-away countries, but the general concern was to focus on developing the subject and the discipline. To be a part of one of the world's centers of the social sciences was to have one's intellectual horizons extended and continually challenged. I may not have been trained in the Social Sciences or in the study of International Relations, but my interest in China and East Asia led to my having to engage with the key concepts and theories of those disciplines, including the role of human agency amid broad based explanations of social change, revolution, history and modernization. These included the concept of Realism and how it may be affected by ideology;

the bases of international cooperation and conflict; the relationships between statehood, governance, and liberal democracy; and the main schools of thought in IR. In other words, I was introduced to a wide world of cosmopolitan modes of thought, which far exceeded the more parochial concerns of much of the scholarship of the Department of Politics in Southampton. Yet I owe much to that department for giving me the opportunity to become an established academic, able to teach and carry out research within the discipline of Political Studies.

I was well treated in the IR Department. As in my first year at Southampton University, I was allocated a first-year class in IR 101, which ensured I became familiar with the main schools of thought in the subject and their various strengths and weaknesses. The LSE at that time had a tutorial system in which university teachers saw their students individually and set them essays over and beyond their class presentations. I encountered students from a wider range of countries than in Southampton and soon became familiar with the problems many had in adapting to life in a foreign major city, especially if they had left the comforts of family living for the first time. Fortunately, the LSE had good facilities for helping students suffering emotional distress. Although tutorials could be time consuming, they enabled me to get to know the students assigned to me fairly well.

In my first year at the LSE, I was allocated supervision of a PhD student for the first time in my life. It was a task I accepted with some hesitation, as I had not completed my own PhD at SOAS a good few years ago – an experience I put down to the lack of proper supervision. The head of the LSE Graduate School, the redoubtable Dr. Anne Bohm, understood my situation and assigned me a mature student to supervise his thesis on China and the Middle East, neatly combining two geopolitical centers in which I had interest. The student, Yitzhak Shichor from Israel, was well prepared for the thesis and the further research he required. In addition to reading and commenting on his draft chapters, my main contribution was to suggest different perspectives on the thinking that underlay Chinese approaches to a part of the world which was apparently far removed from their immediate contact or strategic interests at that time. But my principal concern was to encourage him to develop his own ideas further. Dr. Shichor went on to become one of the world's leading experts on the subject – and especially of Sino-Israeli relations.

During the course of my thirty years at the LSE, I went on to supervise many more PhD students, some of whom also became renowned experts in their respective fields. In fact, supervising research students became the most pleasurable part of teaching. The supervision would start by my encouraging a student to reconcile his or her interest in a topic with the pursuit of a researchable theme. This entailed persuading the student to frame the topic in terms of a question or of a problem that could be addressed through research. Once that was settled, I, as the supervisor, would generally know more about the topic and its ramifications, but as the student delved more into the subject and its research materials, the student would gradually acquire more detailed knowledge and understanding of the topic and its significance than I. Encouraging a student to acquire that kind of academic maturity was one of the more rewarding aspects of being a supervisor. I would end-up learning much from PhD graduates.

Meanwhile, I was frequently invited to comment on China and developments in East Asia on the BBC and other broadcasting organizations in the UK and overseas on both radio and TV, and I became known as an expert on the subject. In 1979, not long after Mrs. Thatcher became Prime Minister, the new

Chinese President, Premier, and General Secretary of the Communist Party, Hua Guofeng, led a delegation to visit Britain. To my surprise, I was among the academic specialists invited to a state reception in White Hall. At around 8PM, all the VIPs disappeared to go to an opera at Covent Garden, but suddenly Mr. and Mrs. Thatcher returned to the reception. Apparently, they were not opera fans. At that point, I was in discussion with a senior BBC administrator of the World Service. Mrs. Thatcher happened to approach us, and the senior BBC administrator began to complain to her about the reduction of the annual contribution by the Foreign Office to help support the World Service, which she had personally advocated.

The Prime Minister stopped him in mid-stream to declare in a high voice, with her arms akimbo, "the trouble with you is that you invite communists to appear on your progammes!" (a reference to leftist commentaries on the Portuguese language broadcasts in support of the recent revolution in Portugal). While the BBC man was caught off-guard, I intervened to say that one of my Chinese students had complained that he couldn't hear the BBC in Peking (apparently the transmission was weak). In response to my intervention, the Prime Minister declared, "What! They can't hear the truth in Peking!" She then turned to one of her minions behind her and bellowed," Take a note of this! They can't hear the truth in Peking!" She was obviously oblivious to what she had just said a moment earlier.

My years at the LSE benefited greatly from working together with the great scholar of Southeast Asian politics, Professor Michael Leifer, in leading a joint graduate seminar on the international politics of the Asia-Pacific from 1973 until his death in 2001. He was more versed in IR theory than I, and his deep knowledge of Southeast Asian history and of the politics of the various countries was exceptional, buttressed as it was by his having taught and supervised many of the members of the elites of those states. In many respects Michael was my mentor, and I owe him an intellectual debt for the care he took in helping me write the first edition of a textbook on the international politics of the Asia-Pacific of 1996. That met the demand for a suitable textbook on the subject. Such success that the book and its revised editions have enjoyed has owed much to his encouragement. More important, as we shall see in a subsequent chapter, the rewriting of additional editions contributed greatly to my intellectual development. But for the present, it is sufficient to note it expanded my research and writing beyond a focus on China to turn to developments which shaped the Asia-Pacific as a whole. That helped me to place the significance of China in a wider context, and it freed me from becoming too Sino-centric.

It was a joy to be a member of the IR Department. Not only was it one of the first of its kind in the world, but after the Second World War it was at the center of the development of a distinctive approach to the subject, known as "The English School". This regarded international relations as less of a system and more as a society of states, that was sufficiently flexible to accommodate other forms of organizations, but it was a society characterized by its own rules and norms. As a theory, the English School was close to classical realism, but it was more attentive to the importance of international law and norms. Indeed, it has been recognized as incorporating the concept of morality into realism. The key progenitors of the English School had already moved on by the time I joined the Department in 1973, but their influence remained.

Nevertheless, not all members of the Department adhered to The English School. The Department was composed on the whole by headstrong figures, some of whom were intellectual leaders of their respective branches of the IR discipline. It would be invidious to single out some as opposed to others, but among those who influenced me greatly was the afore mentioned, Michael Leifer. Others included Philip Windsor, Adam Roberts, James Mayall, Susan Strange, Fred Halliday, and Chris Hill. Perhaps what illustrates best the distinctive character of the members of the Department in the course of my thirty years' membership, unlike most academic departments, was how well we all got on with each other. There were neither major schisms nor personal animosities, such as were evident in some other departments at the LSE, or in other IR departments in the UK. Such disagreements or personal dislikes that existed in the Department were kept within bounds and did not reach levels which poisoned the atmosphere.

My Mother's Family

The move to London brought my children and me into closer proximity to my parents, who two or three years earlier had moved from an apartment into a spacious house with a garden in Wimbledon. By this stage, my father, who had qualified as a solicitor had his own office in Clapham Junction. After helping him settle in, my mother was finally able to retire after five decades of work as a secretary. Thus, my arrival coincided conveniently with my mother having the time to spend with her grandchildren, as well as to cultivate a truly beautiful garden.

My parents also now had the opportunity to accommodate members of my mother's family, who visited London as part of their tour of England and Europe, especially at a time, when travel to and from the other side of the world was becoming easier and more affordable. We were all struck by their refreshing openness and straightforwardness in contrast to the complexities of most Europeans and Middle-Easterners we had generally encountered.

My mother's family was from Christchurch in New Zealand's South Island. Her father, recorded in the name of "Mr. Tom Tankard, aged two", migrated to Christchurch from England as a passenger in one of the famous "Four (Sailing) Ships", which helped to establish the city in the 1850s. He went on become the champion cornet player in New Zealand and the leader of a well-known brass band in South Island. He made his living as the owner of a bicycle shop. He fathered four daughters and a son. His son-in law, Peter Mahon, became a high-court judge. Peter had served in World War II, mainly in Italy. He stayed several times with my parents in the early 1970s, entertaining us with his dry wit. Later he became internationally famous for his finding in the enquiry into the crash of an Air New Zealand flight on Mount Erebus in 1979 on a tourist sightseeing tour of Antarctica. Contrary to an earlier finding that put the blame on pilot error, Judge Mahon found fault with the airline for having changed the flight coordinates the evening before the flight took off without informing the pilots. He famously accused the airline's executives of having issued "a litany of lies". Unfortunately, the judge was pilloried by the airline and by the New Zealand Prime Minister (aka "Piggy Muldoon") and it is thought that the strain led to his early death. In the end he was fully exonerated, and his investigation became a model for subsequent investigations of air disasters.

Another well-known relative, Sam Mahon, the son of the Judge, also spent some time at my parent's house in the mid-1970s. Of a different generation, Sam was a budding artist and a non-conformist, eager to find things out for himself. He has since become a famous artist in the South Island, with sculptures adorning towns and public gardens. He has become active in seeking to prevent the pollution of farmland, the rivers, and underground water supplies for grazing areas. He has had no compunction in criticizing and lampooning local officials for allowing the destruction of the country's land.

On a more personal note, my move to London with three young children occasioned a second marriage, which was arranged in undue haste with the aim of not unsettling the children through the uncertainties of a live-in 'girl-friend'. As it happens, the second marriage ended sooner than the first, in part because my children and she did not get on and in part because an activist trait in her character made her seek to commit herself to the Chinese cause of the late Cultural Revolution – as she saw it. She was able to stay on during a visit to China in the spring of 1976, and we were divorced two years later.

The China Factor

On returning to London I quickly found myself as a leading commentator on China's politics and foreign relations, especially for the BBC's World Service, which was then located at Bush House in the Aldwych in London, just across the road from the LSE. Chinese politics were then at a turning point, as China's leaders were engaged in a power struggle to determine the fate of the Cultural Revolution and the imminent succession to Mao Zedong. The struggle was taking place against the backdrop of immense changes in international politics as the Vietnam War was winding down amid the continuing antagonism between China and the Soviet Union, the emerging conflict between China and Vietnam, and the emerging uncertainties of China's alignment with the United States.

My arrival at the LSE coincided with the arrival of about eight students from the People's Republic of China assigned to study in the School's International Relations Department. Apparently, Mao Zedong and Zhou Enlai were struck by the relative youth of the diplomats and aides who accompanied Richard Nixon and Henry Kissinger on their visits to Beijing. China's diplomats still belonged to the generation who had been recruited in the 1940s, some of whom had been active as journalists and Communist Party representatives even in the 1930s. The training of diplomats in the 1950s had been deeply influenced by the Soviet system and had been largely discarded in the 1960s due to the rift with the Soviet Union. The trainees of the 1960s had never been abroad and had been deeply affected by the xenophobic Cultural Revolution. Moreover, many of those who had attended foreign language institutes had been Red Guards whom Mao had sent down to the countryside in 1968. The example of the young American diplomats made Mao and Zhou aware of the generation gap in their coterie of diplomats. Given China's relative isolation and deficiencies of knowledge of foreign languages, future diplomats were first trained in foreign language institutes. By the end of the 1960s, virtually all of them had been sent down to the countryside. Due to the perceived need to recruit a new generation of capable diplomats, many of these 'sent down students' were rapidly summoned back to Shanghai and Beijing in 1971/72, and, after a short training about living conditions in the West, they were dispatched to "improve their English" for two years to those English-speaking countries which had full diplomatic relations with Beijing. The first port of call was the UK, where in the first year more than a hundred were sent to Atlantic College in Wales and to Ealing Polytechnic in London. The British Foreign and Commonwealth Office reached an agreement with the newly opened Chinese embassy that between eight and ten of these students, chosen by the embassy, would spend their second year at the LSE.

As the only specialist on contemporary China at the LSE at that time, it fell to me to supervise their studies. They fitted in as General Course students, designed for students staying for one year only. Such students did not have to take formal examinations, and that accorded with the anti-examination ethos of the Cultural Revolution, which was still current in China. General Course students were also allowed great flexibility in choosing up to four subjects on which to receive lectures and to participate in related classes for group discussion. It fell to me to allocate tutors for them. At that time the LSE had a tutorial system, which in addition to classes and lectures, facilitated the supervision of students on a personal basis. In other words, tutors could see their Chinese students separately without being monitored by their fellow Chinese students. That not only facilitated the treatment of students according to their separate needs and interests, but it also meant that – perhaps for the first time in their lives – they could speak freely without concern of being monitored by Communist Party members or other official representatives. To be sure, it took a little time for them to adapt to this system and to build trust in their tutors. They also had to adapt to new forms of teaching and learning, in which there was no view or interpretation deemed to be the only 'correct' one. Nor was there an emphasis on learning by rote. In fact, their initial reaction to being confronted with more than one way of interpreting events was to ask their teacher which was the correct one. Perhaps the new 'freedom', which won immediate support, was their gaining open access to all the books and journals in the LSE library (one of the world's most comprehensive in the social sciences). Nothing was forbidden to them and they soon learned to use brown paper as covers for the books as a means of hiding the title from unwanted on-lookers.

One of their most important experiences stemmed from being housed in general student dormitories, rather than being located in apartments or rooms belonging to their embassy. They benefited from the opportunities to interact with LSE students drawn from all parts of the world. That being said, it is important to bear in mind that they saw themselves as representative of their country and they behaved accordingly. They tended to dress in variants of 'Mao suits' and were a rare site on the streets of London in those days of the 1970s when there were hardly any people to be seen from the People's Republic of China. But life was not always easy for them. In their first year in the UK, they were often assigned to live with local families, who sometimes treated them with condescension, even though it was well meant. For example, they were told how to use the bathroom or knives and forks. Also, it was not always easy for them to adapt to life in London. One female student told me how difficult she found travelling in the London underground (or Metro) at first. Coming from China, where at that time women wore no make-up and everyone wore the same drab khaki or blue shapeless clothes, she was taken aback by what she saw as the garish make-up and colorful, stylish clothes women in particular wore, and it took several weeks before she could distinguish between her fellow commuters.

Beginning in the spring of 1974, the students would come to my apartment on a Sunday in April at around 10 in the morning and prepare a meal, which entailed their taking over the kitchen and using nearly all the cooking implements, so that 3-4 hours later we would share a virtual banquet. However, on one occasion something went wrong: they turned up at lunchtime unannounced, with no preparations having been made for any cooking. I took them out to a nearby Turkish restaurant, explaining that this was the kind of food that ethnic peoples (or national minorities) in China's far west tended to eat. They had never eaten such food, but they could hardly refuse without appearing to be unpatriotic in disparaging a Chinese 'national minority'. The Turkish restaurant manager was surprised and delighted to entertain his Chinese customers dressed in Mao suits, the like of which he had not seen before, and promised to prepare his best dishes. They were duly delivered to the table, and as I started to eat the delicious food, I noticed that my Chinese friends were abstaining. I quietly asked one of them what was wrong. He then sat upright and assumed a dignified position as he declared to me, "we Chinese people do not eat sheep!" I explained to the manager, and he replaced the offending dishes without further ado. Since then the eating of lamb and mutton has become widespread in China. But I was struck by the tendency then of even sophisticated Chinese to speak to foreigners as if they were doing so on behalf of all Chinese, of their tendency to overlook 'national minorities' as fellow citizens, and to regard the Chinese identity in ethnic or racial character (i.e., as Han Chinese)

Additionally, I was struck by the insularity of especially those students who came in the first two years (1973-75). On one occasion, two of them were reminiscing about their experiences on being sent down to the countryside. A young woman related how her group was attempting to store grain in a huge empty room in a house, when an old man with a beard who was concerned about possible damage to his 'special books' obstructed them. At that point, a male student interjected to ask how her group reacted, as he asserted that, in his view, the old man was wrong to try and block the interests of the village. When I suggested that the room may have been a place of Moslem worship and that the 'special books' may have been Korans, the two looked mystified. Apparently, they had never heard of Islam before. Later students tended to be more knowledgeable. Some of them also told me of their

94

experiences. One had been sent to the far north near the Soviet border to "confront the revisionists", as he put it with a degree of irony. Moreover, he complained of being poorly equipped for the extreme cold of the winter weather. A female student once told me it was sometimes so cold in her student dorm in the North-East (aka Manchuria) that she and others would stay in bed sometimes for days on end just to keep warm.

For me, the encounter with these students was like a breath of fresh air. Instead of the turgid ideological language of Chinese official writings or the exaggerated accusations of Red Guard tabloids, I found thoughtful reasonable people seeking to explain Chinese political developments in sensible terms. Thanks to them, I was able to follow many of the twists and turns in the last travails of the Cultural Revolution, which officially came to an end after Mao's death in September 1976 and the arrest of the 'Gang of Four' a month later. However, I was surprised by their general lack of interest in British society and politics. They seemed to be interested only in things to do with China. When I took them to the British Museum or to art galleries, they displayed no interest in cultures other than China's. Roderick MacFarquhar, who was then an MP, invited one group in the mid-1970s and another the following year to attend debates in the House of Commons. The students seemed astonished to see leading politicians such as Mr. Edward Heath and Mrs. Margaret Thatcher in live action in plain sight before them. But they never once asked me about that. Perhaps their reticence was because it was inconceivable that any of the Chinese leaders would be on public display like that, and that they did not wish to be embarrassed.

The students all came from foreign related official institutions and ministries and although some of them had been Red Guards in 1966-68, none could be said to sympathize with the Chinese 'left' by the time they came to the LSE. Most, but by no means all, were children of the political elite. Their annual studies at the LSE came to an end in 1979 when the new Prime Minister, Margaret Thatcher, raised the fees for overseas students at British universities to new heights. The end also coincided with the establishment of formal diplomatic relations between China and the US. The US had always been the preferred destination for Chinese officials and students. Additionally, American universities at that stage were eager to admit Chinese students and offered them scholarships and preferential admission rates, with which the LSE could not compete.

In time, many of the Chinese from the LSE rose to high positions in Chinese foreign-related official institutions. At least three started as official interpreters for China's most senior leaders on returning to China. Many later became ambassadors, at least three became Chinese representatives to the UN and went on to become ambassadors to Washington. Another was the chief negotiator for China's entry into the World Trade Organization, and he was subsequently honored by the LSE. Four became Vice Foreign Ministers and at least one became Foreign Minister, a State Councilor, and, at the time of this writing, he is a member of the Political Bureau of the Chinese Communist Party. I have been entertained by some of them to exquisite dinners on many of my subsequent visits to China. On being asked about their experiences at the LSE, they were impressed by the freedom allotted to them to read anything they liked. Some acknowledged the challenge of having to develop independent modes of thought.

Australian Interludes

While I was still at Southampton University, I was invited in 1972 to attend and to contribute a paper to a conference in Australia on the opening of China to the outside world. The conference took place shortly before the Federal election was due and which the Labour Party was expected to win after many years of conservative rule. The changes in China's international position, caused by the rapprochement by the Nixon administration, contributed to undermining the policy positions of the conservative government. The eagerness for change was palpable at the conference, and I gained some understanding of the brashness of the style of Australian politics.

At the same time academic life was conducted with great seriousness and professionalism. Perhaps that was a consequence of the self-consciousness of being at great distance from the West and of the perceived need to be accepted and appreciated in England and the United States. Some Australians dismissed this attitude as a product of "the colonial cringe". The assertiveness of the left in 1972, which had been aroused earlier by opposition to the Vietnam War in the late 1960s, included a reaction to that deference towards Britain and America.

On the way back to the UK in 1972, I stopped off in New Delhi, where the British embassy arranged for me to give a public talk on China. Despite it being ten years since the war with China, the hard feelings of defeat and humiliation were still very much in evidence, and my attempt to take a relatively neutral position between China and India was not well received. I had to be rapidly withdrawn from a side door.

In 1976 I had occasion to visit Australia again. As mentioned earlier, there were problems with my second marriage and we thought we might be able to overcome them, if we were to take a break from England. I secured a six-month fellowship at the Australian National University in Canberra, beginning in January 1976, which would also allow us each to pay a three week long visit to China in April. My China visit, as a member of an academic group called "young British Sinologists", was arranged through the British Council. That was my first visit to China, which I shall discuss later on. My wife's separate visit, arranged through a group of the Society for Anglo-Chinese Understanding (SACU), began a little earlier in April. In the event, that trip provided the occasion for our ultimate separation. She was so enamored with what she found in China that she found a way to stay there as a polisher of English translations for the Chinese Foreign Languages Press.

I thoroughly enjoyed my relatively brief stay in Australia, but it took place under a very different political climate from the one I saw four years earlier. The Labour Prime Minister, Gough Whitlam, whose government had carried out a social-democratic agenda of reforms in the intervening years, had been dismissed by the Governor General (the Queen's representative) amid a constitutional crisis just a couple of months before my arrival. There were bitter recriminations and the political atmosphere had turned sour. However, coming from England, I came to appreciate the rawness and openness of Australian discourse. The fact that the Queen's representative had dismissed Whitlam removed much of the earlier deference, but some replaced that with what might be called resentment or a kind of chip on the shoulder. However, one of the appealing characteristics of Australian culture was the readiness to accept people without regard to their social positions or pretensions. The ideal of "mateship" may be taken too far at times, but it embodies a central core of (male) Australian attitudes. In short, I found much to appreciate in both the optimistic times of 1972 and in the more bitter times of 1976.

Chapter 7: My first visits to China

After that first visit in 1976, the door to subsequent visits to China seemingly opened and I visited yearly or every other year for over four decades. These visits to interview officials and fellow scholars exposed me to the uncertainties of life in a dictatorship that had something of the character of totalitarianism. At times, the dictatorship was looser than others, and people were allowed more opportunities to express their opinions. These times were subject to the constraint that at some point they would be limited once again, with harsh consequences to those deemed to have transgressed. There were no clear rules, so there was an arbitrary quality to the dictatorship. There was a built-in incentive to be cautious. That applied especially to Chinese citizens and indirectly to foreign visitors such as myself. I used my words with greater care than usual in order to avoid causing potential trouble for my interlocutors or interviewees. For that reason, I very rarely cited the name of such an individual in my articles and books.

It was not my place to raise possible difficulties for them. The result was that I continually found my visits to China stressful, and I was full of admiration for those Chinese academics who took the risk of challenging the authorities.

The general effect, however, was to enhance my cosmopolitanism. I became less willing to pass judgment on people, and I tried to take greater care in making efforts to understand why they expressed particular points of view, or indeed why some chose to withhold expressing one at all. I became more tolerant and found myself becoming more empathetic towards people whose views did not necessarily accord with mine. Early in the course of my visits to China, it became apparent Chinese scholars and officials were prepared to convey their personal views as distinct from official viewpoints mainly when they were alone with me. Very rarely would they speak out in the presence of another Chinese interlocutor. I soon learned that public discussion of sensitive topics, such as what it meant to be Chinese – was it primarily defined by ethnicity, culture, geography, or ideology – was frowned on. Similarly, the question of why official interpretations of Chinese recent history continually changed could only be broached once considerable mutual trust had been built with the Chinese interlocutor, even when our discussions had long been confined to ourselves without the presence of a third person.

At the same time, the experience of living, however briefly, under the dictatorship of the Chinese Communist Party (CCP), sharpened my own liberal views, though I did my best to avoid expressing them in an offensive way unless I deliberately sought to provoke a response. Let me give an example. In 1996, I was a member of a group of European scholars who were seeking to explore with Chinese from foreign affairs institutions how best to improve mutual relations. At the outset, it was agreed I would talk about Hong Kong, as that was the most important issue in Britain's relations with China. After the almost deferential talks of my European colleagues, my talk struck a more discordant note. My theme was why the British public was uneasy about the impending handover of Hong Kong to China. I then recounted all the various incidents in which the CCP had caused the deaths of millions of innocent Chinese people, culminating in the Tiananmen massacre of June 4, 1989, and I pointed out that the CCP had never stated how many had been killed nor had it apologized for the killings. My European colleagues looked daggers at me for supposedly undermining the purpose of our visit. The Chinese present responded by saying the British should indeed feel uneasy because of all the horrible things they had done to the Chinese people in the hundred years beginning with the Opium War, and each Chinese scholar and official took turns pointing out several such incidents. However, as we were leaving the meeting, a number of the younger Chinese (including those who had denounced me) approached me quietly and congratulated me for saying things they hoped would be passed on to their leaders. In any event, I continued to be invited to China, and Chinese officials continued to solicit my views.

On my first visit to China in April 1976, as with all visitors in those days, I was a member of a group. My group consisted of a dozen or so scholars of contemporary China, between 30 and 40 years of age and under the auspices of the British Council, who had been invited by the Chinese Ministry of Education as a delegation of "young British China scholars". The visit coincided with the last major political struggle of the Mao Zedong era. At issue was the question of the succession to Mao and whether it would lead to a continuation of the ultra-leftist policies of the Cultural Revolution, under the leadership of Mao's wife and her associates (aka "The Gang of Four"), or put an end to revolutionary politics and turn to policies of reform and economic modernization under the leadership of Deng Xiaoping.

The struggle was sparked off on the night of April 5, 1976, when the Beijing militia (under the control of leftists) forcibly removed the thousands of people and the many wreaths from the Monument to Revolutionary Martyrs in Tiananmen Square. The incident took place on the day on which Chinese people marked the Qingming Festival by sweeping their family graves. Those arrested had been protesting for several weeks against the regime's deliberate policy of keeping to a minimum any mourning for Premier Zhou Enlai who had died in January. This was the first time that ordinary Beijing citizens had openly and spontaneously protested against the regime. Zhou was regarded as a moderate and was called the "People's Premier", but for the previous two years he had been criticized by Mao and his Cultural Revolution stalwarts (later pilloried as the "Gang of Four") for allegedly seeking to reverse the Cultural Revolution and to give priority to modernizing the economy. The April 5 incident led to the dismissal of Deng Xiaoping three days later and to the attempt to pursue leftist Cultural Revolution policies, principally in education, culture, industry, and agriculture. Mao died on September 9, bringing to an end the leftism of the Cultural Revolution.

Although I was very much aware of the ongoing top-level political struggles which had been taking place in China for the previous few years, I was also very much excited to be able to visit the country for the first time after studying it from afar for 17 years. Like many others who had been opposed to the American war in Vietnam, I was prepared initially to suspend my doubts about the claims made by the (leftist) Chinese authorities about the new policies adopted in the wake of the Cultural Revolution. My attitude was affected by the readiness of our hosts, the Ministry of Education, to allow our visit to go ahead the day after the confrontation in Beijing, involving the first-ever spontaneous mass demonstration against the authorities since the communist state was established in 1949. In fact, our group had assembled in Hong Kong the day before and were shocked to wake up on April 5 to read vivid accounts in the Hong Kong press of the violence in Beijing overnight. We wondered whether our visit would be allowed to go ahead as planned. But we were able to cross over by the well-trodden bridge from Hong Kong to the then market town of Shen Zhen with a population of around 20,000 (which has since become a huge city of over 12.5 million). We were well received there and after a brief delay we were whisked off to a local museum, where we were kept for several hours. It took us less than half-an-hour to see what the museum had to offer and we were uncertain whether our projected tour might be called-off. Suddenly we were summoned to a mini-bus containing our luggage and driven to the airport, onto the runway, where we boarded a plane whose engine was already running, and we took off late at night to Beijing. The other passengers on the plane were mainly soldiers, who loafed around the seats without paying the slightest attention to the stewardesses or to safety features.

On arrival, we were driven through a largely empty city to its one tall building at the time, the Beijing Hotel, located on the main Beijing thoroughfare, near the famous Tiananmen Square. Although it was nearly midnight, a few of us walked to the Square, which was surrounded by soldiers with fixed bayonets, a yard or so apart, yet we could see that the center of the Square was being hosed down. Over the next two days there was an atmosphere of tension as none of our Chinese minders was prepared to tell us what was going on. On the third day we awoke to the sound of drums and general excitement: Deng Xiaoping, it was announced, had been dismissed, from office, but he was still allowed to retain his

103

membership in the Communist Party, which suggested he had not been totally disgraced, even though he was accused of being the mastermind behind the pro-Zhou challenge to the authorities. In the following days, we saw a series of people marching to the Square holding banners of their institutions supposedly demonstrating their anti-Deng feelings. But we could see that the vast majority was unenthusiastic, and many looked as if they were just going through the motions.

The organizers of our visit took us to see universities, notably Peking University, where we were introduced to students drawn from workers, peasants, and soldiers and to a few of their older professors. The latter claimed unconvincingly to have benefited from their experiences of working with peasants in the countryside, from whom they said they had learned a great deal. They also repeated the current propaganda line of the value of teaching and learning from the new kind of students. In one of the suburban communes of Beijing we were told by a middle-aged peasant in vivid language of the advantages of operating in a collective unit and were regaled with statistics of enhanced production to prove the point. We also visited an iron and steel factory, which to my untrained eye, was not marked by great activity, as many workers seemed to be at rest, while many materials were strewn about to no apparent purpose. Nevertheless, a worker outlined an account of the organization of the factory and presented statistics, which apparently indicated high levels of production. We were taken to a kindergarten, where we were entertained with a song and dance by the toddlers with the motif of criticizing Deng Xiaoping. We were also taken to see a 'revolutionary' Peking Opera and to other song and dance performances.

Later, we were also taken to many famous tourist sites, including the Great Wall, the Forbidden City, the Hutongs (walled alleyways) of old Beijing, and other such sights. We had plenty of time to wander about by ourselves. I had the opportunity to visit Yang Xianyi and his wife, Gladys, who were well known in England as translators of Chinese literature, spanning from the classics to the contemporary. I shall have more to say about them later, but, on this occasion, they had sought me out to say that my wife (who had been a member of an earlier group of 'friends of China') intended to stay on to work for the Foreign Languages Press.

My impression of Beijing was mixed. I was impressed by the enormous effort to show off the apparent achievements of the Cultural Revolution, but I felt much of what we saw was propaganda akin to 'Potemkin villages'. Beijing itself in those days was a city of walls which concealed much of interest. For example, the famous hutongs were narrow passageways between walled off compounds, which were closed to those on the outside. In those days, the city was crowded with bicycles, and, in the early hours, you could see 'honey carts' led by donkeys, as human waste was taken from households in vats to fertilize the fields just beyond the city. The main problem, however, was the caution with which people spoke to each other and especially to foreigners. It was clear every neighborhood and apartment block had monitors (usually older ladies) whose job it was to report on anything deemed suspicious, including any encounters locals may have had with foreigners. I felt then and in the subsequent forty years of visiting the country that I should use my words with care – not so much on my behalf, but to ensure that I was not causing difficulties for any of my Chinese interlocutors. It was only when I left to return to Hong Kong that I felt free of that pressure and could fully relax.

From Beijing, our group went by train to the Yangtse towns and cities of Yangzhou, Nanjing, and Shanghai. Despite the fraught politics that were never far away, I appreciated the relative openness of these cities, which, unlike Beijing, were not the centers of state officialdom and whose passage ways and were not defined by enclosed walls. From there, we went south to the countryside around Guangzhou, where I was greatly impressed to see traditional methods of breeding silkworms and the making of silk. The people of the region, the Cantonese, seemed different from their kinsmen to the north. It was as if frenzied politics was not as big an issue for the Cantonese.

In sum my first visit was both exhilarating and troubling. Like all first-time visitors, I was greatly impressed by the famous sites of the Great Wall and of Beijing, the other cities, the rivers, and the countryside. Yet the pollution in April was much worse than I had expected: the wind blew from the interior, carrying both industrial dust and dirty fine loess sand from the deserts in the interior. The social effects of the political dictatorship were clear to see. People were careful in what they said and in how they behaved. Even the clothes they wore tended to be dreary olive green and blue jackets and trousers, conveying the sense that no one was willing to stand out with a personal touch, let alone style.

My Second Visit

In the summer of the following year, 1977, I made an altogether different visit. Mao had died, the 'Gang of Four' had been arrested and Hua Guofang, Mao's designated successor, was nominally in charge – until the formal re-emergence of Deng Xiaoping the following year. Meanwhile, something of the residue of the Cultural Revolution remained, as Hua was committed to upholding "whatever" Mao advocated. Hua and his associates were the beneficiaries of the Cultural Revolution, in the sense that they had been singled out for promotion. They could hardly disavow Mao and his Cultural Revolution without undermining their own legitimacy. Perhaps that was why Hua pledged to adhere to "whatever Mao said". Hua and his associates were progressively sidelined as "whateverists", enabling Deng to consolidate his leadership.

My (second) wife had elected to stay in China, working for the Foreign Languages Press (FLP) and, as her husband, I was allowed by the terms of the Chinese contract to spend three months with her. By the end of my visit, it became clear our marriage was coming to an end because she was intent on living in China, whereas I was committed to pursuing my life as an academic at the LSE and to being a father to my three children. Nevertheless, my three months in China were very rewarding in many respects, putting me in touch with a good number of those foreigners who stayed in China in the 1930s and 1940s and who contributed to propaganda work to the outside world. I got something of a glimpse into the working of the FLP and other propaganda outlets. I also made early contact with Chinese academics.

I stayed with my wife at the 'Friendship Hotel', which was then just on the outskirts of the city. Happily, my 12-year-old son, David, joined me for the last few weeks of my stay and we explored Beijing together by bicycle. The Friendship Hotel was a huge complex built by the Russians in 1954 to house the Soviet experts who had come to help modernize China. It was walled off from contact with ordinary Chinese, and it was broadly self-sufficient with its own amenities such as a large swimming pool, tennis courts, restaurants, etc. By the time we stayed there, the Soviet experts had long been withdrawn to be replaced in the 1970s by Western experts on temporary contracts. Longer-term residents included those Western communist sympathizers who had lived in China since the 1940s (and some even from earlier times). The complex was also beginning to serve as a normal hotel for visiting foreigners.

I got to know a number of the long-term residents, all of whom had suffered imprisonment and worse during the Cultural Revolution and had received an apology from Premier Zhou Enlai. Some remained fervent supporters of the Chinese authorities, even as the ideology and policies changed. They were sometimes derided as "sunshiners", because they always claimed that the situation in China was excellent, as if the country were always bathed in sunshine. But there were some who continued to adhere to the leftist position of previous years. It was difficult not to feel sad for these foreign sympathizers, who were kept apart from most Chinese in their privileged 'Friendship Hotel'. Some of them had had access to the top leaders, including Mao himself, but they were never able to integrate fully with ordinary Chinese. It was as if they had been elevated to a high position, where they were located in a kind of no-man's land, or in a limbo, where they were formally designated as "friends of China" and yet kept at arm's length distance. Less than a handful eventually became citizens, but that was more an honorific position than one which placed them in the same situation as normal Chinese citizens. At the same time, most of them felt alienated from their original homelands. Some had gained distinction in academic and official positions in America and the UK before openly joining the side of the Chinese Communists.

One such person was the economist and spy Solomon Adler, whom I got to know, and he was nostalgic for his encounters with distinguished economists at the LSE from his years in Cambridge in the 1950s. "Eppie" Epstein, was a different character, who traced his communism to experiences in the East End of London and was married to an aristocratic lady (Elsie Fairfax Cholmondeley), an avowed communist. Epstein was devoted to the Chinese communist cause. He claimed expertise on Tibet, on which he wrote three books, which followed the Communist line of portraying the Party as liberators. Others at the Friendship were a motley crew, who doubtless were sincere adherents of Chinese communism and who faithfully adhered to the abrupt changes in the Chinese communist line – until Deng Xiaoping disavowed Mao's policies, when many were torn between clinging to what Mao stood for and to embracing Deng's reforms. In any case, by the late 1970s and after Mao's death, their previous role as propagandists was no longer needed, leaving them to reflect on their past as historical curiosities.

In the days before the reforms began to make their mark, urban Chinese people belonged to work units. The Communist Party leaders of these units (Danwei) controlled much of the lives of the resident workers, including whom and when they could marry, where they could live, when and how many children they could have, and what education would be available to them and their children. Similarly, the Danwei would provide their healthcare and pension, and it (or rather the Party secretary) would determine the character of the furniture to which they were entitled. Notwithstanding the loss of privacy, urban registration was much prized, as various amenities and provisions were available only to official urban residents. Travel beyond one's immediate environs was strictly controlled, requiring letters of official approval. If these restrictions may have seemed onerous, those for rural dwellers were even worse. Not only were they confined to their places of residence, but their villages and townships were supposed to be self-sufficient. Their consumption was limited to what they could produce – but only after submitting the required quota (set at a low price) to the state. Unlike their urban counterparts, they were not entitled to a regular income supplemented by rationing. Their health care was limited, and, they became dependent on their families in old age. Educational opportunities were limited more often or not to primary school or to low-level middle school.

Like the other visiting foreign spouses at the Friendship Hotel, my Danwei was limited to where my wife worked, and, in my case, it was the Foreign Languages Press (FLP). But unlike our Chinese colleagues, we were not subject to the same degree of control of our lives by local Party leaders. I was able to become friendly with a good number of people at the Hotel and at the FLP, but nearly all the Chinese I knew maintained a discreet distance. The effect of Maoist social controls – and especially of the upheavals of the Cultural Revolution – was to erode trust between Chinese people and to enhance the sense that unless it was a requirement of your work, it was better to avoid contact with foreigners, as that usually led to trouble.

The following may serve as an example. In the summer of 1977, a rumor suddenly surfaced in the Friendship Hotel and in the FLP that an attempt had been made on the life of the Hollywood actor, William Holden, who was then staying briefly at the 'Friendship'. It transpired, according to the FLP that a man had been detained for breaking into the grounds of the Friendship, where he assaulted a foreigner, one of Holden's entourage, with a knife. But no real harm had been done. It transpired that the assailant was a man from NE China, who had a grievance against local officials for maltreating him and his family. Unable to get redress, the man traveled to Beijing with the intent of attacking a Westerner. At that time, Westerners were treated with kid gloves and the assailant knew his attack would be thoroughly investigated by the higher authorities, which he hoped would lead to redress for his family, even if he were to be executed for his crime.

The most significant Chinese relationship I developed was with Yang Xianyi and his wife, Gladys. Xianyi was an Oxford graduate in Classics (i.e., ancient Greek and Latin literature) and Gladys, in 1940, was the first person to graduate in Chinese at Oxford. Xianyi was an ardent patriot, and the two returned to China after their marriage to contribute to the Chinese resistance to the Japanese invasion. The two remained after the Communist victory, hoping to contribute to the 'New China.' Together, the pair translated classical and modern Chinese writing into English. Xianyi became a famous intellectual, and their home in Beijing became a meeting place for Chinese artists and writers of all hues. In particular, their home welcomed students, writers, and intellectuals from England, especially from the 1970s onwards. Xianyi was dubbed affectionally, "England's son-in-law". But they and their family suffered terribly in the Cultural Revolution. The two experienced several years in isolation in prison, their only son committed suicide, and their two daughters went through hard times, as well. Nevertheless, Xianyi maintained a cheerful disposition. He loved to drink Chinese spirits and Scottish whisky and to smoke with his artist and writer friends and with his European visitors. Both Xianyi and Gladys used to poke fun at my reports of interviews I had with Chinese officials. Their home was a welcome place of refuge for me from the daily grind of contact and interviews with officials. Most of my evenings were spent there with their European friends, talking, drinking, and singing well into the night.

In addition, I think it was through them I gained access to the famous artist Huang Yongyu. The authorities wanted to publicize him in the West, as evidence that Chinese art and true artists had survived the Cultural Revolution. Due to my broadcasts on China in London, I had been selected to try and make his art known to Westerners. A commentary by my then-wife and me was published with photos of his work in the (London) *Sunday Times* of January 15, 1978. I was fortunate to be given a large painting of lotus flowers signed by the artist and dedicated by him to my (second wife) and me. I even have photos of him actually painting the picture. In the 1960s, he had painted a picture of an owl with only one eye open. In the early Cultural Revolution, Huang was criticized by Mao's wife, Jiang Qing, for painting an owl "with one eye closed on socialism". She included Huang Yongyu's paintings in an exhibition of so-called 'Black Art'. He was detained in a tiny room, and, in a mood of rebellion, he painted huge paintings through the device of folding the large paper into smaller parts. He was released after the fall of the 'Gang of Four'. My article displayed photos of his woodcuts and paintings, including his huge painting of the landscape of China, which was displayed as the backdrop to the entrance to Mao's Mausoleum in 1977. I asked him once, given his free and independent spirit, how he coped with the control of culture by the Chinese Communist Party. He replied by telling me the story of a mother with a difficult child who did not want to board the train to go home. He threw himself on the floor and refused to move. The mother then began to make her way to the train and the little boy then wiped away his tears of rage and followed his mother. He had to follow her, as he had nowhere else to go. In other words, the painter had no alternative. But in due course, Huang settled in the freer domain of Hong Kong.

In the summer of 1977, I went with a few service people from the hotel to see an international football game between China A Team and North Korea. Before the start of the game, there was a surprise announcement that Deng Xiaoping had joined several other leaders attending the game, in his first public appearance since his dismissal the previous year. In the first half of the game, the Chinese side appeared to score a goal, but the North Korean team disputed it. They lay down on the pitch and refused to play any further. The referee was at a loss and began to walk towards the special stand of the leaders. The Chinese captain followed him in hot pursuit, signaling it was no goal. Meanwhile, the newly installed electronic scoreboard frantically flashed "Friendship First, Competition Second." Play resumed, the game ended 1:1, and the crowd dispersed quietly. On the way back to the hotel, I told my astonished companions that had that incident occurred in England, there would have been a riot, and the Korean players would have been lucky to leave the stadium unscathed. A year later, I heard that Hong Kong had defeated the Chinese team in a world cup qualifying game in Nanjing, which led to a riot and to physical attacks on anyone who looked like a foreign Ethnic Chinese (Overseas Chinese). It was a sign that the Chinese fans had indeed joined the modern world.

Later that summer, I was invited by the leaders of *China Literature*, a journal of translations selected by the Communist Party-approved editors, to provide an opinion by a Westerner of the stories. Although I criticized some for their propagandist character, I'm afraid I disappointed the Yangs and their more liberal-minded colleagues, who wanted a more blistering critique and complained I was too mealy mouthed. On another occasion, I was taken to see a Peking opera with the theme of an emperor of the 9th century marrying-off one of his daughters to a Tibetan ruler. This was based on a true historical event, in which the Chinese sent an imperial princess to Lhasa as a kind of hostage in order to placate Tibetans, who at that time were strong enough to pose a threat to the emperor and his capital city. But the play presented a mythical theme of the condescending civilized Chinese bestowing honor and friendship on Tibetans, who were depicted as wild barbarians. It so happened that the following day, I interviewed the then-editor of the Peking Review (now the Beijing Review), the weekly news journal for the outside world. In response to my observation that the play disparaged the Tibetans and ignored all they had contributed to Chinese culture, the editor turned to one of her deputies to answer me, because, she said, he had recently returned from a stint in Tibet. After a pause, he said they had contributed some medicinal herbs. Nothing was said about their cultural contributions.

I had asked my hosts to arrange for me to meet a foreign-affairs official to discuss China's policies towards the Middle East and other matters. I had almost given up, when towards the end of my visit, I was taken to meet a senior "responsible person". He then proceeded to give me the official account of the basis of China's foreign policy, but when pressed on the Middle East and on Israel specifically, he distanced himself from the PLO and some Arab states saying, "we have never said that the Israelis should be driven into the sea." I was delighted, thinking I had been told something new. But it turned out this had been China's position for some time.

By this time, I was regarded almost as a member of the FLP work unit, and I participated in a visit to Da Zhai, Mao's agricultural propaganda model. It was in a barren hilly country in which the peasants, supposedly under inspired leadership, transformed the unpromising land into a thriving agricultural community with their bare hands through enthusiastic labor. Da Zhai had become a Maoist showplace, visited by millions of people. Unfortunately for the local leadership, one of whom had been elevated to the high post of Vice Premier, Da Zhai was shown to be a sham not long after Mao's death. Far from its much-heralded achievements being the result of amazing hard work, resilience, and self-reliance, they were shown to be the result of hidden subsidies and special favors.

Further evidence of the deceptive character of much Chinese propaganda was the way in which fabrications were deliberately foisted upon foreigners. For example, as a supposed friendly expert at the Friendship Hotel, I was approached by an official of the China Official Tourism Bureau to check the English translation of the presentation

114

local peasants and workers had to make to visitors about their work units, as if these were their own words. In those days, the places open to foreign visitors were strictly limited. I took the opportunity to check the presentations my group had been given in the visit of April 1976, and, lo and behold, the statements and production figures given by gnarled peasants and calloused workers came back to me almost verbatim. Yet at the time, the presenters seemed authentic and entirely convincing.

Subsequent visits in the 1970s

The following year, in 1978, I got myself invited to the newly opened Chinese Academy of Social Sciences (CASS). Until the onset of the Cultural Revolution in 1966, the few social sciences covered in China were modeled on Soviet practice and incorporated within the Academy of Science. Now, however, a different approach was to be followed, although, to start with, a distinction was still drawn between institutions primarily engaged in research and those primarily engaged in teaching. I offered three lectures in the hope the rest of my two weeks could be spent in interviewing officials and scholars. On arrival, I found my hosts wanted nine lectures. We compromised at eight, which demonstrated my poor negotiating skills. Feeling somewhat resentful of the extra work and of the more limited time I would have for interviews, I titled my first lecture, 'why the West Europeans were hesitant to ally with China against the Soviet Union.' But rather than explain why the Europeans wanted to pursue détente, I launched into an attack on the Chinese as unreliable allies. Comparing alliances to marriages I listed the half dozen or so Chinese alliances made since 1949, all of which had broken down with the Chinese heaping all the blame on their erstwhile allies. I then went on to say a friend might accept their account of the first two breakdowns of a marriage, but doubts would creep in at the third and be confirmed by the fourth, fifth and six, by which time they would be seen as unreliable allies. An awkward silence descended on the room, and, not being used to such silences, I interjected other points, which led to a stilted discussion. My other talks were less confrontational and more acceptable, as I tried to explain the standard theories of International Relations taught at British universities.

The following year, in 1979, to my surprise I did not get a favorable response to my request for another scholarly visit. In fact, I didn't receive a reply at all. I enquired of my friends the Yangs, and eventually it transpired that my second wife, from whom I thought I had been amicably divorced, had persuaded the Beijing diplomatic representatives of the Palestinian Liberation Organization to make an official request that my proposed visit be cancelled. Apparently, she had claimed a self-identified Zionist such as I should not be invited. Rather than make an issue of it with the PLO, the Chinese authorities withheld my invitation. Thinking that under these circumstances any letter I wrote to the Yangs would probably be opened by the Chinese authorities, I wrote a complaint and added I was sure other Western scholars would be interested to learn their being granted a visa to enter China would be conditional on their not taking a favorable attitude towards Israel. Within a month or two, I got a letter of invitation from the relevant institute inviting me to come in 1979.

However, that was not quite the end of the matter. On arrival at Beijing airport, there was no one from the institute to greet me, as was the normal custom. I then took a taxi to the nearest Western Hotel (the newly opened Lido) and explained the matter by phone to Yang Xianyi. He advised me to present myself to the institute the following morning, which I did. I was received warmly by the head of the institute, who then arranged for me to give several talks and to conduct a number of interviews. At the first talk, the head took the unusual step of introducing me to those attending, beginning with a representative of the municipality and continuing with those from the police, the public security organization, various foreign related official institutions and other institutes of CASS. Without saying a word about the earlier failure to reply, the head told me of the significance of the attendants, which I took as indicating that I was now regarded as a foreign scholar of good standing, hinting in the process that he disapproved of the previous denial of a visa.

Clearly, the Chinese were beginning to move away from the Cultural Revolution and leaders of educational institutions were no longer afraid to counter decisions by higher authorities deemed to be unjust. Another example of the new reformist atmosphere in which people were prepared to take decisions as individuals against the prevailing norms was the readiness of young women to wear colorful clothes. That may seem a trivial example, but in fact it was an example of people choosing their own life styles in defiance of officialdom. The era of reform had truly begun. The lesson for me was how the apparently insignificant degree of change in a totalitarian system can portend great new developments.

It was in that context I got to know some of China's leading specialists on international relations, who later became well known as advisers to the government and Party leaders. They also became known as senior academics and as interlocuters between China and the West. In that capacity they were frequently interviewed by journalists and quoted by the international press. This was also true of leading academics in other Asian countries. In particular, in Japan I got to know some of the leading Japanese specialists on China and more generally on Japan's foreign relations. As it was in Japan's relations with Korea, so it was with Sino-Japanese relations;

scholars on both sides got on well together, without enmity, regardless of the ups and downs of relations between the countries concerned.

Chapter 8: The Last Two Decades of the 20th Century

The 1980s were a period of both reform and reaction for China. There was a continual struggle at the top of the Communist Party hierarchy between reformers and their opponents. It was a period marked by alternating patterns of what the Chinese called "loosening" and "tightening", which culminated in the public demonstrations in many Chinese cities, notably in Beijing's Tiananmen Square – the symbolic center of the Communist regime. The mass demonstrations began in April 1989, opening all too brief a period of uncensored public discussions in the history of the PRC. It ended in the massacre of citizens and demonstrators on June 4, 1989 by the misnamed People's Liberation Army.

The 1980s were years of excitement for young Chinese especially and, of course, for students of Chinese politics, such as myself. It was in 1980 when the reforms really began in one of the poorer parts of the countryside, where peasants reverted to family farming at the expense of the Communes system of collective agriculture. Productivity grew, enabling small-scale markets to develop and locally related village manufacturing enterprises. The local senior official, who was an associate of Deng Xiaoping, encouraged these efforts. Families came to hold the equivalents of leases for 15 years. That gave them a stake in the longer- term development of the land and for technological and market related improvements. That reform came to be called "the responsibility system", which then became the model for the whole country.

The urban sector also underwent reforms. In the early 1980s, my academic interlocutors were encouraged to purchase their apartments at extremely favorable rates. Some of them went on to upgrade them to new apartments in recently built modern high-rise buildings. The 1980s were a period in which older buildings, including many of the famous Hutongs, were demolished to make way for modern high rising buildings. A few people objected to being displaced, mainly due to the break-up of long-lasting communities. But most, including my academic friends, welcomed the move to contemporary apartments with modern facilities such as built-in toilets, running hot water, modern appliances, and the freedom to choose their furniture, etc., but above all to be free to have a higher degree of privacy. It was only then that local friends invited me to their homes.

On the political front, I was able to visit "Democracy Wall" to the west of Tiananmen Square, where, in early 1980, students and others were able to paste a new kind of 'wall poster' (unlike those of the Cultural Revolution) demanding political change. The most famous was Wuer Kaixi, a dissident Uighur from China's far west, who had put up a long wall poster calling for democracy and which openly criticized Deng Xiaoping by name. Initially, Deng tacitly allowed the liberal views expressed by such wall posters to stay, but he soon reacted against them, doubtless encouraged by more orthodox fellow leaders, and issued an injunction against criticism of the Party and requiring adherence to its ideology. The tightening of permitted views soon went too far. Some of the activities of the Cultural Revolution returned, going as far as cutting people's hair in public and getting people to resort to the 'proletarian' clothes of the 1960s and early 1970s. Soon, however, the new criticism of unorthodox views was deemed to have gone too far. A new spirit of reform returned.

My encounters with academic friends were not greatly affected, except some of the heads of their institutes were changed in accordance with the prevailing political tide. At one point, during a time of tightening, one of my friends, who was destined to reach more senior positions, complained about the amount of time taken-up by Party meetings, but the fact he confided in me in this way indicated he did not take the events too seriously. It seemed as if they were more of a nuisance than a precursor of a serious clamp down to come. These were times of transition and uncertainty, typified for me by meeting with a young person from among Premier Zhao Ziyang's circle of advisors. Her enthusiastic commitment to the cause of reform was not matched either by experience or by familiarity with the different reforms in Eastern Europe. Yet what she lacked in expertise was soon overcome by her commitment to the reforms.

As demonstrations at universities across the country became more frequent, the orthodox, or conservative, leaders became more troubled, and, in 1987, they managed to have the reformist Party General Secretary, Hu Yaobang, dismissed from office, although he was still allowed to attend meetings of the Politburo. It was at one of these meetings in April 1989 that he suffered a heart attack, which killed him shortly afterwards.

Dissatisfied with the low-level attention given to the way he was being memorialized, students in Beijing demanded more be done to mark his achievements. Their protests led to the beginning of the Tiananmen demonstrations, which lasted for over two months in the full view of television from Western countries. The demonstrations ended in a massacre by the Chinese army of hundreds and perhaps two thousand or more young people shown live on Western television sets.

Yang Xianyi, the public intellectual famous for his translations of Chinese literature, later gained esteem in Western circles for his open denunciation of China's leaders on the BBC for the Tiananmen massacre of students on June 4 1989. At the time, such open dissent was punished severely. Fortunately, Xianyi, who had gone into hiding, was not detained.

The 1980s were a period of political change in several East Asian countries. The Marcos dictatorship in the Philippines was replaced with a parliamentary system with some of the characteristics of democracy, although the traditional elite families continued to hold on to considerable political power. Thailand, too, was shedding some of the aspects of military rule, as the 1980s saw a gradual momentum towards democracy. These developments influenced students in China. That in itself demonstrated the degree of change in the region. Now that the region was more open, young people followed what was happening elsewhere, and their expectations drew encouragement from sprouts of democracy in neighboring countries.

While many of my academic friends participated in the demonstrations in Beijing, none was killed or badly injured in the massacre by the 'People's Liberation Army'. They varied in their attitudes: some were critical of the lack of organization of the demonstrators and the lack of clear demands for change, while others, who had been abroad – particularly in the US, the

UK, Australia, France, and Germany, participated and tried to focus the protests on achievable demands. In the end, it was all to no avail, as the movement fractured into competing groups. Nevertheless, this was the first time Chinese people discussed political and other views openly. Even journalists from the leading Party newspaper, *The People's Daily*, took part in the demonstrations, denouncing the lies they had to publish. The elderly communist leaders feared for the survival of the Party and the regime. In the words of Deng Xiaoping, "we cannot retreat any further with our backs to the wall." The Party leaders were divided between reformers and the hard-liners. The former were associated with Zhao Ziyang, the Party General Secretary, who was soon placed in house arrest until he died 16 years later. The Party veterans headed by Deng Xiaoping, who ordered the military to shoot the demonstrators, prevailed. My friends favored reform and therefore kept a low profile. But when I visited Beijing about a week later, the quiet anger and dismay of Beijingers was palpable. A youthful bookseller at one of the main bookshops encouraged me to buy books by reformers, because in her words, "they [unnamed] would soon ban them".

A few months later, the East European communist states began to overthrow their communist leaders. China's rulers tried in vain to support their East European equivalents. By this stage, the other Chinese leaders held Deng Xiaoping and his reformist policies responsible for the debacle of the Tiananmen massacre and sought to revert to Stalinist-style command economics. Meanwhile, Deng and US President G.H.W. Bush were reaching an agreement to restore full diplomatic relations. At a central Party meeting at the end of December, Deng was able to get his comrades to endorse his agreement with America and his new push to restart the reforms. He overcame his obdurate opponents in Beijing by undertaking a highly publicized tour of China's southern region opposite Hong

Kong and Taiwan to establish special economic zones to take advantage of the proximity of the capitalist knowhow of the neighboring fellow ethnic enclaves. Since communism had long lost such appeal as it may have had to the Chinese people, Deng began to emphasize nationalism, or what was translated into English as "patriotism", as a means to galvanize the people – and the young in particular – to support his efforts to modernize the economy, improve people's standard of living, and build the country to be strong enough to resist external pressure. In fact, the economy grew by over 10% throughout the 1980s, far exceeding the projected rate of the conservative socialist model. Some of my academic friends began to act as advisers to certain leaders, but it was amazing how soon the majority accepted the new order with materialism and nationalism as the new banners, instead of communist ideology.

It so happens I met my third wife, Ellen, in February 1989, and she began to follow events in China, in part because I was continually in demand by broadcasters. We married the following year and celebrated our thirtieth anniversary in November, 2020. Ellen and I visited China quite often in the 1990s and the first two decades of the 21st century. I would conduct interviews and hold discussions with academics and officials, and she would take notes almost verbatim. As a lawyer (solicitor) in England, she was practiced in taking notes of court proceedings for barristers. Her notes for me were practically word for word and, above all, they were legible. In that sense we were a team.

Southeast Asia

The 1980s turned out to be a good time for the ten members of the Association of South East Nations (ASEAN). Through diplomatic means, they successfully resisted Vietnam's attempt

124

to consolidate its conquest of Cambodia and, despite the misgivings of Malaysia and Indonesia about isolating Vietnam, ASEAN established itself as a diplomatic community. ASEAN took the lead in successfully pressing the members of the United Nations and other international Institutions to oppose Vietnam's occupation of Cambodia. The members of ASEAN had different strategic interests and were divided by overlapping ethnicities, religion, and historic differences, but they operated by consensus and by the agreement not to interfere in the domestic affairs of other members. Far from being a regional community or an alliance, its members could not even come together as a group to help members confronting national disasters. They were all post-colonial states, which prized their national independence and were seeking to consolidate their fragile governmental systems.

Much of their respective domestic politics and foreign policies were not publicly revealed, not so much as a passion for secrecy or for reasons of political culture, but for self-protection. First, with China as a neighbor, they all had reason to avoid giving offense unnecessarily. Second, that was also true of their management of relations with each other, though their different ethnicities and religions often spanned their borders and had to be handled with care. Third, there were mutual animosities arising from history and from the colonial era, and care was necessary to avoid reviving them. Take Singapore as an example: a maritime city-state which was expelled from the newly formed Malaysia in 1965, in the expectation it would flounder. Instead, Singapore flourished, as may be gauged from the title of a book by its founder, Lee Kuan Yew, *From the Third World to the First*. From the outset, it attracted international companies and Western governments, not only for economic reasons, but also because Singapore was successful in promoting itself as an international city. Populated mainly by ethnic Chinese, it presented itself as a multi-ethnic and multi-cultural city, lest its neighbors – and China in particular – should regard Singapore as a "third China", after Taiwan. Its much larger immediate neighbors, Malaysia and Indonesia, are predominately Moslem and tend to regard Singapore with jealousy, claiming it allegedly enriched itself at their expense. Much of Singapore's defense orientation is to protect itself from them. After all, there have been anti-Chinese riots in each of these neighbors, which could easily have spilled over the border into Singapore.

I first visited some of the Southeast Asian countries in 1979, and the main topic for discussion with academics and a few officials was China. I was surprised to find out how few specialists they had on China itself, as opposed to the Overseas Chinese in their midst. In the 1980s, I saw the number of specialists grow, mainly as the result of attending universities in Europe, Australia, and the United States. As an example of the lack of domestic expertise or because of the sensitivity about China, as an outsider, I was invited in 1986 by the Institute of Strategic and International Studies in Malaysia to write a monograph on the 'Chinese threat.'

The 1980s was also the decade when I traveled extensively in Northeast and Southeast Asia, interviewing officials and scholars and taking the weekends off to visit sites in the various countries. I made many friends throughout the region, but in general I found more warmth and openness in SE as opposed to NE Asia. Perhaps this may be explained by their respective historical experiences. Both Koreans and Japanese were rather insulated and proud of their distinctive cultures. They also entertained bad feelings towards each other stemming from their pre-modern entanglements, as well as from the experience of the Japanese invasion and occupation of Korea in the first half of the 20th century. Traditionally, China had protected Korea from Japan, but Japan had defeated China in 1895 and invaded it in 1931. It was evident from the National Museum in Seoul that South Koreans felt more sympathy towards China than Japan, despite China's invasion of the Korean peninsula after the American defeat of the North in 1950. An uneasy stalemate was reached in the summer of 1953, when an armistice was signed and a de facto border was agreed on between the North, supported by communist China and Soviet Russia, and the South supported primarily by the United States. There was great animosity between North and South Korea, as both regimes swore to reunify the Korean peninsula by overcoming the other. At the same time, however, there was no evidence of mutual enmity between their respective scholars in the several conferences I attended over the forty years since 1980. Nevertheless, both Koreas feel intense antagonism towards Japan, which had annexed Korea in 1910 and tried to replace Korean culture with its own, until the defeat of Japan in 1945. The animosity towards Japan in the South and Japanese disdain for Koreans continues to this day, notwithstanding the fact that each is allied separately with the United States, which treats them as strategic assets in maintaining the American role in East Asia. For my part, I have strong friendly relations with academics on both sides of the divide, and especially with former Korean and Japanese PhD students

I visited most of the Southeast Asian countries in the 1980s. In contrast to the peoples and officials of NE Asia, I found the SE Asians far more open and welcoming. I did not feel there was some kind of unbridgeable gap between local and Western people, as there was in China, Korea, and Japan. Perhaps the latter could be explained by the restrictions of Communist Party rule in China and by the historical and cultural insularity of Korea and Japan. The Southeast Asians, by comparison have been engaged in international trade since ancient times. Whatever the reasons, the differences between these East Asia sub-regions are palpable. I was also struck by the prominence of female political analysts and International Relations specialists in the main research institutes and think tanks in SE Asia. However, I must emphasize I encountered nothing but pleasant treatment and warm hospitality by all my interlocutors in Asia, despite the many differences between all the countries, the sub-regions of countries, and the residue of anti-colonial feelings.

I found Singapore to be the most congenial of the regional cities. It was the least polluted, its academic standards were equivalent to the principal universities in the West, and its officials were the most open. Moreover, English was the official language. I most admired the way it dealt with its vulnerability. It successfully resisted the continual pressure from the Chinese state to incorporate Singapore within its own political culture. Many Chinese from the mainland failed to understand the difference, so it was a continual problem. Even Chinese leaders tended to think that because about two thirds of the people of Singapore were ethnically Chinese, they could expect the Singaporean government to show special deference towards them and allow them the latitude to intervene in domestic Singaporean affairs. For example, the former Singaporean Ambassador at Large, Bilahari Kaukisan complained openly of various ways in which Chinese officials interfered in the country's domestic affairs.

The Philippines, by contrast, was most disappointing. After the Second World War (or the Pacific War) it was judged by the IMF to be best suited among the countries of the -sub-region to be an economic success. Instead it has fared most poorly in comparison with the other founding members of ASEAN. It has more in common with Latin American countries than with its SE Asia neighbors. It was a Spanish colony for 300 years and although Spanish is hardly spoken any more, the Spanish legacy is still apparent. Some 80% of the population professes Catholicism and it has entrenched elite rural families with their land holdings and private militias. These families control a large proportion of the economy. The Filipino experience as an American colony has been less beneficial than that of the British, Dutch, and French colonies in the region. The political independence of the Philippines occurred as early as 1946, but it was not until about 15 years later it regained full legal economic independence. It has the façade of democracy, with a few families dominating political power. A quarter of the more than 100 million population is below the UN poverty level, yet the Philippines has high rates of literacy and an expanding number of students in tertiary education. The shortage of available employment means many find employment abroad, and in the first decade of the 21ˢᵗ century, the average contribution of remittances to the country's GDP exceeded 10% a year. A sad joke I encountered in Manila of the 1980s was, "Go home Yankee, and take me with you!"

Indonesia, as the largest country in Southeast Asia, has been the unofficial leader of ASEAN, but it has been careful not to assert that leadership, in order to assure smaller members their respective interests would not be overlooked. Officials and members of think tanks have been careful not to be seen as over-bearing. Nevertheless, I have found them uninhibited in explaining their country's views and policies. For example, in the 1980s, during the Vietnamese occupation of Cambodia, the underlying view of the military – as explained to me privately by a senior military officer – whose leader General Suharto was then in power, was that the main enemy of SE Asia was China and not Vietnam. In fact, the military felt a degree of solidarity with its Vietnamese equivalents, because both their armed forces were perceived to be central to their respective struggles for independence. In order to ensure the unity of ASEAN and its diplomatic efforts to delegitimize the

Vietnamese occupation, Indonesia went along with the other members. Indonesia was primarily a Moslem country, although 13% of the population professes other faiths, and the founding documents of independence claim adherence to "Pancasila", whose five principles include a call for belief in the Almighty without any mention of Islam. Further, the majority of Indonesians still adhere to a tolerant form of Islam, which includes the legacies of earlier religious practices. Although Indonesians generally sympathized with the plight of the Palestinians, I found no prejudice whatsoever against me as a Jew.

Malaysia is also a Moslem majority country, with just over 60% of the population professing Islam. 20% of the population is Chinese, and there is a history of animosity between the two ethnic groups. There is also a government policy of discrimination in favor of the Malays. Yet as a visiting academic in the 1980s, I encountered little of that. Like the Indonesians, there was more concern about the possible threat posed by China than by Vietnam. But unlike Indonesians, the Malays were more troubled by the possible impact of China upon the ethnic Chinese within the country. There was no love lost in the Malaysian regard for Singapore, a fellow member of ASEAN, which had been expelled from Malaysia back in 1965, and I encountered a view that Singapore's economic success was due to its taking advantage of its two immediate neighbors. As for relations with China itself, Malaysian officials were optimistic about the growth of China's economy – from which they hoped to benefit – but distrusted it as a political and strategic partner. The academics with whom I spoke said officials were divided between those who support a partnership with China and others who sought to maintain a certain distance from their giant neighbor. But in the American view, Malaysia was still a strategic partner.

Thailand was the only SE Asian country not to have been colonized. It had been a buffer between French ruled Indo-China and British ruled Burma. Thailand was a constitutional monarchy, with the main political power held by the military, balanced by weak political parties that were essentially personality led patronage groups. I first visited Thailand in the 1980s, when the country was ruled by technocratic governments effectively controlled by the military, with occasional interventions by the King. After political turmoil in the previous decade, the 1980s saw significant economic growth and the beginnings of modernization. As the frontline state in the conflict with Vietnam, Thailand played a key role in galvanizing ASEAN to deny legitimacy to the Vietnamese imposed government in Cambodia, and it was the principal conduit for supplying arms to the three groupings contesting Vietnamese forces on the border. By the time I first visited Thailand in the summer of 1984, the conflict at the border with Cambodia had basically stabilized, and the Thai economy was prospering.

The Thai government was engaged in subtle diplomacy: On the one hand it was quietly helping China funnel military supplies to the Khmer Rouge remnants, who offered the most effective resistance to Vietnam, while also keeping Indonesia and Malaysia engaged with ASEAN in the policy of isolating Vietnam. As noted earlier, Malaysia and Indonesia regarded China and not Vietnam as the main threat to regional order. The Thai diplomats and the second track participants, with whom I discussed the difficulty in ensuring that the two doubters of ASEAN's diplomacy on Indo-China would not break the common position, were aided by Vietnam's intransigence on the issue.

I did not visit other SE Asian countries until the 1990s, however, the diversity in each of the countries and between them and those I visited in the 1980s made a deep impression on me. I saw the futility of European visitors attempts to persuade the members of ASEAN to adopt the European model of a regional grouping. These were countries which had only recently gained independence from colonial rule. Each was seeking to consolidate independence and establish new political systems under a surge of their respective nationalist movements against a background of mutual distrust and a history of enmity. The various countries had to find their own ways of maintaining a balance between the major external powers – primarily China and the United States. They were neither interested in, nor capable of pooling sovereignty on the European model, and they lacked the institutions or modern economies to do so. In fact, one of the leading Western experts on SE Asia published a book in 1979 called, appropriately enough at the time, *Region in Revolt*, yet within a few short years, most of the countries had achieved a degree of order to embark on significant economic growth and shake off Western attempts to bind them to external influence. In short, they had become masters of their own fate. Their diversity in terms of political culture and historical experience enhanced my sense of cosmopolitanism.

Chapter 9: American significance in Asia is challenged in the 1990s

The 1990s are usually seen as indicative of the economic rise of China, but I have chosen to emphasize the American side of developments in Asia. What many of my interlocutors among America's regional allies in East Asia regarded as a series of self-inflicted wounds by the Clinton administration came about in its treatment of China. Having gained the presidency in part by accusing his electoral opponent, G.H.W. Bush, of "coddling tyrants from Baghdad to Beijing", President Clinton promised to deny China normal trade tariffs until it improved its human rights. In the event, under pressure from American business, he gave way in 1994 and reversed his policy. Two years later, in 1996, the Chinese attempted to intimidate the Taiwanese on the eve of their first ever election of a president by firing missiles near its two main ports. Clinton's response was to send two carrier-led battle groups to the area, but only after forewarning the Chinese side. That sign of 'toughness' was very soon followed by Clinton's reaching out to the Chinese leader and arranging for mutual state visits.

Once the Asian Financial Crisis erupted in July 1997, the American side did relatively little to provide assistance, and it went out of its way to praise the Chinese side and to condemn the Japanese even though the latter had given $44 billion to the affected SE Asian countries, whereas China had given only $4 billion. In fact, the overall Japanese contribution more than doubled that of America. In that year, I was told by one of the Chinese regional specialists in trade that the crisis was the fault of Japan for having devalued the Yen months earlier. In fact, the Japanese did not devalue their currency but did the opposite in September 1985, when the yen's value was raised by about 50% as part of the Plaza Accord, involving the U.K., Germany, and France, as well as Japan and the U.S. But the explanation for the crisis given by Western economists was that the affected countries had borrowed in US$, but once their local currencies had lost value, they were unable to pay back the loans in US$ when the repayments became due. The Chinese refusal to devalue their currency was much appreciated in the region and beyond, even though a senior Chinese official admitted that it was not in China's own interest to devalue. The favorable treatment of China by the Clinton administration may be seen as derived from the enthusiasm with which most Americans greeted the rapprochement between Nixon and Mao in 1972 and China's strategic partnership in managing relations with the Soviet Union. Beyond the pragmatic calculations, successive American administrations were influenced by the long term significance for Americans of what they saw as their role in guiding China towards democracy and active participation in managing the international system. This somewhat romantic vision is a legacy from the 19th century. Having seen at first hand the terrible treatment of Chinese people by the Chinese Communist Party and the disdain with which the CCP held many of its neighbors, I did not share the romantic view that many Americans had of China.

In the autumn of 1997, my wife and I visited Beijing, when I was invited to teach for one term at the China Foreign Affairs University attached to the Ministry of Foreign Affairs. This was among the elite universities, and it trained students to become future diplomats. I was to teach on Chinese foreign policy, but I decided to focus on what I took to be the foundational blocks of the foreign policy, beginning with three weeks on China's international identity, followed by three weeks on what it means to be Chinese. I talked for the first half hour and then we spent the next hour of every class on discussion. The students were also required to write two short essays over the 12- week course. I told them I did not want a repeat of official accounts; instead, I wanted to hear and read their own views of the various topics. After an initial hesitation in accepting that there was no necessarily one correct view among the explanations on offer, they all took to their tasks with enthusiasm – except for one, who was introduced to me as the student representative of the communist party. He said he had to correct my 'erroneous' views and therefore presented the official account, allegedly for my benefit. Collectively, we had lots of fun, and the deputy director of the university told me our class was the most popular among the students. One confided in me that before the massacre of June 4, when the students from the main universities to the north passed by the Foreign Affairs University, they called out to the FAU students to join their demonstrations. This was more than seven years since any mention of the Tiananmen events was totally taboo!

On my various visits to China, I often met with previous students, many of whom had attained senior positions in government. One of them arranged for my wife to help teach English to taxi drivers and medical personnel at a Chinese traditional medicine hospital. They were people who were expected to work with foreigners in the course of the Olympic games due the next year (1998). My wife had never taught before nor had she ever used a digital slide presentation. She was only told the day before she was expected to teach the following day. Imagine her trepidation when she was suddenly thrust into a lecture hall with over a hundred taxi drivers. She talked to them about her breakfast, drawing pictures on the blackboard. All went well, which gave her confidence to go and address the medical personnel. She gave talks about the various American special days as they came due, including Columbus Day and Thanksgiving. In her preparations, she discovered what she had learned at school bore no relation to the real people and the actual events celebrated back home. My wife did so well that in the end she was given the award of a "model worker" – an award which is much prized in China.

In 1998, President Clinton visited China for his longest overseas foreign trip. Unusually, he did not take the opportunity to visit Japan, as well, which was resented in Japan, especially as Japan was the long-term ally which was totally dependent on America for its security. In Japan, it came to be called "Japan passing." During the visit, Clinton also became the first US president to assert publicly that America did not support membership for Taiwan in any organization for which sovereignty was a condition of membership. In addition, President Clinton managed to upset New Delhi by pledging to press jointly with China for India and Pakistan to walk back from the nuclear brink by halting all nuclear tests. Not only did New Delhi take umbrage at the implication that Beijing and Washington would jointly manage South Asian security issues, but Japan was none too pleased by signs that China and the US sought to exercise joint management of Asian security affairs. Academic think tank personnel in both Tokyo and New Delhi conveyed these views to me.

As already noted, the US did little to help the Asian countries directly affected by the economic crisis of 1997, other than refer them to the IMF. American behavior during the crisis reduced its standing in the eyes of many in Asia, and its preferred financial model of the free market, known as the 'Washington consensus', was discredited as a panacea for all economies, whether developed or not. Ironically, the Asian crisis took place just as the World Bank issued an official report on the Asian "economic miracle", praising some of the countries most affected by the financial crisis. The Clinton administration not only praised China excessively, but it also went so far as to turn down Japan's proposal for having an 'Asian Monetary Fund'. It had been apparent for some time that many Japanese had been disenchanted with its ally. An early indication was the 1991 book, *The Japan That Can Say No*. The Japanese academics and officials with whom I discussed these issues at that time maintained the book went too far. But they were apprehensive the United States might be more inclined to favor China over Japan, which would leave Japan isolated diplomatically, having to develop an independent defense capability, and some Japanese hinted their country might have to develop its own nuclear deterrent. In the event, Sino-American relations soured somewhat in the late 1990s. Although Japanese fears of abandonment abated, they didn't entirely disappear, leaving a degree of distrust in Japan which led Japanese governments continually to seek reassurance from their American ally. My talks with academics, journalists, and officials confirmed these concerns, and they indicated a high degree of wariness about China and a distaste for Korea. A very senior official of the Japanese Ministry of Foreign Affairs told me in November 2017 South Korea was "the Finland of Asia". The map on his office wall showed Japan as a group of islands in the Pacific along with Taiwan, the Philippines, and the South Pacific islands. South Korea and China were not represented on the map. This kind of expression of nationalism was not congruent with Japan's national and strategic interests, in which the alliance with the U.S. was deemed to be crucial. From a cosmopolitan perspective, these developments demonstrated the fragility of contemporary alliances based mainly on strategic concerns between governments, without being underpinned by close affiliations between the respective peoples.

Southeast Asian countries plus South Korea felt the impact of the financial crisis most. In fact, it led to the overthrow of Indonesia's long-term leader General Suharto. Arguably, his downfall was the result of domestic discontent, but his fall was symbolized by a famous photograph of the leader of the IMF standing over Suharto in 1997, as he signed the document of acceptance of a loan. The episode was marred by anti-Chinese rioting in the capital and beyond, with China being unable to offer protection. However, these events opened the way to establishing a degree of democracy. This was soon followed in 1986 by the fall of President Marcos of the Philippines, when he lost the support of the armed forces and the Catholic Church. He was exiled to Hawaii, where he died in 1989. The Philippines, too, turned to democratic elections.

By the time of the late 1990s, the Southeast Asian countries were beginning to recover from their financial crises, and Myanmar, Vietnam, Laos, and Cambodia had been admitted into ASEAN. Nevertheless, long held animosities persisted, even though institutional progress had been registered on the economic front. I was still struck by the tendencies of Western politicians and leaders to regard ASEAN as akin to their regional associations. But ASEAN had neither the inclination nor the capacity to behave as a coherent international actor. Even in the economic sphere they tended to be competitors, making true economic integration difficult. The growth of the Chinese economy increased its importance for the economies of the region. But the smaller Southeast countries became more apprehensive of their giant Chinese neighbor, even though they were careful to limit the expression of such views in public. China had registered extensive claims for islands in the South China Seas, as well as for most of the Sea. Some of these were contested by maritime neighbors, who were confronted with this huge neighbor asserting its claims were "incontestable", even though they were not recognized in International Law.

The sheer diversity of these East Asian countries, in terms of histories, political cultures, political systems, affinities and enmities, geography, sizes of population, religions, levels of economic development, and so on, both deflated my senses of cosmopolitanism and, paradoxically, also encouraged them. Despite the incipient conflicts, the region has been free of warfare for forty years. That is not necessarily the consequence of closer interactions between the peoples, except perhaps for the common institutions and the closer economic interactions of the countries of ASEAN, but it may be the consequence of mutual nuclear deterrence between China and the United States and the huge destructiveness of even conventional wars. However, mutual deterrence is not necessarily stable and the prospect of low-level conflicts or skirmishes is very real. These could lead to escalation and unintended consequences. Moreover, all the countries are experiencing nationalist movements of varying intensity. These, of course, are not conducive to the development of cosmopolitan sensibilities. As far as the Chinese Communist Party was concerned, from the outset and continuing through all its seven decades in power, America has been regarded as the principal enemy, which sought to weaken and undermine the Party and change the regime.

Chapter 10: America and the Need for Cosmopolitanism

After my retirement from the LSE in 2003, I moved to the United States, where, thanks to my friend and colleague, Professor David Shambaugh, I was appointed a "Visiting Scholar" at the Sigur Center for Asian Studies at the Elliott School for International Affairs, George Washington University in Washington, DC. I chose Washington for two reasons. First, the Washington area contains more experts on China-related issues such as politics, economics, history, foreign policy, strategy, anthropology, demography, climate change, health, etc., than in the whole of Europe. Moreover, European governments have been primarily interested in economic relationships with China, as they have long since ceased to be a factor in the balances of power in the region. The second reason is that my third wife had two grown children living in the Washington area, who were soon to be married. I had a married daughter, Tamar (Tammy), living not too far away in New Jersey. My other two children, Daniella and David stayed in London, as did their three beautiful daughters, Rachael, Aisha, and Omi.

To return to the main theme of the book, in which I wish to argue for the abiding significance of cosmopolitanism, this is especially true of the current period, which involves the urgency of addressing global problems, such as climate change and disease pandemics. Instead, the general international response is to look at these problems through the narrow and limited lenses of nationalism and populism. At the time of this writing, the world confronts the coronavirus pandemic with no end clearly in sight at least before the summer of 2023-2025. The world's reaction has been to hunker down in the parochial approaches of separate states and nations. Meanwhile the various problems arising from global warming continue to be largely unaddressed, despite the promises of various governments, some of which – notably the United States – have refused to recognize its causes or to accept policies which might have mitigated the damage that was being done, especially during the Trump presidency. He did much to erode existing environmental laws and to support the expansion of the harmful fossil fuel industries.

Given the intensification of problems arising from globalization and global warming, I shall not address the impact of political developments in the first two decades of this century as in previous chapters. Instead, I shall focus more on general issues concerned with global change. Of course, I recognize the significance of America's reaction to "9/11"and to the financial and economic crises of 2008/2009 and their aftermath. Also, I shall assume the reader's familiarity with the effects of America's two longest wars in the Middle East and the American reaction (or over-reaction) to "international terrorism". All of which may be seen as underlying America's relative international decline and the rise of China as a peer competitor of the United States, despite the latter's continuing status as the world's only true superpower.

Having come from London, I shall first consider my reaction to the change of encountering what is still a superpower, after living in the UK – a country seeking to re-establish its independent character after the loss of empire and the rejection of the European Union.

Differences between Washington and London

Washington, of course, was much more than the main Western center for the study of and policy-making towards China. It was the capital of what is still the world's only superpower, with an economic reach spanning all parts of the world and military power surpassing any single or combination of countries. The United States sees itself as the world's most consequential power. It was founded as a people of shared enlightenment values. Unlike most other countries, it does not base its identity on the notions of ethnicity, history, language, traditional culture, or land. The United States was founded on the idea that political power is derived from the people and belongs to the people. It was the world's first contemporary democracy, and, from the outset, its founders recognized the country's exceptionalism and thought of the US as a beacon to the world. However, from its foundation, it has been damaged by the prevalence of slavery. Despite their emancipation after the civil war (1861-1865), severe discrimination against African Americans has persisted to this day. Nevertheless, since its founding, Americans and their leaders have thought of their country both as a model of inspiration and attraction to others and also as bearing a responsibility to encourage and to promote the development of democracy and free markets elsewhere in the world. These two strands of focusing on being a model for emulation ("a city on the hill") and of being active in promoting democratic change have been at the heart of debates about American foreign policy and its role in the world since the country's foundation in 1776. One early American president warned his fellow citizens against searching the world for "monsters to slay", another led the country to its first victory by its standing navy, defeating the Barbary Pirates of North Africa very early in the 19th century.

It will be seen from the foregoing that the United States was founded not only on the desire to be free of British colonial rule, but also by the desire to establish a democratic republic, allowing for a broad degree of freedom for its citizens. In other words, Americans saw their system of government as founded on the basis of certain liberal ideas and principles derived from the enlightenment. The practice of the ideals of freedom, democracy, and the rule of law has had to be adjusted over time to meet the needs of major historical changes, including the huge transformation from a primarily agrarian economy to an industrial one and, more recently, to a post-industrial, mainly automated and service-based economy. These social, economic, and technological transformations have required huge adjustments by institutions and to the way of life of Americans, while remaining true to the principles expounded in the founding documents about governance and the ideals mentioned above. The United States remains the only major country to have welcomed its wartime adversaries into independent states. In the process, it has helped each of the major countries to recover from the destruction of war to become functioning democracies with independent capacities to become major global economies.

Americans have been committed to the prospects of change. Perhaps, as compared to the West European democracies, the United States has placed more emphasis on technology as an instrument of change than on social developments. Moreover, American political culture stresses the importance of future changes, as illustrated by the successful election slogan of a recent American president, "don't forget about tomorrow". In other words, in the main, American society is forward looking. Its system of education and social practice call for the cultivation of leadership skills in order to bring about change. Conservatism in America does not mean to work in alignment with established practice. In the US, conservatism is seen as a more activist force, calling for the enhancement of the free market, keeping the size of governments and their practices to the severe minimum, favoring private enterprise, opposing the organization of labor, etc. From an English perspective, American conservatism professes an activist right-wing ideology, far removed from the more passive character of British conservatism.

Given American political activist tendencies and its yearning for an active leadership role in the world, as allowed by its considerable power, it is possible to project in the distant future for America to lead the way in encouraging the adoption of cosmopolitan outlooks.

Meanwhile the contention between these two schools of thought of isolationism and internationalism has been evident ever since the founding of the state. For example, as the US turned inwards after the First World War, the US Senate rejected membership in the League of Nations, as promoted by President Wilson. Two decades later, President Roosevelt struggled to persuade the American people to join the Second World War, and it was only after the Japanese struck at Pearl Harbor he gained full public backing. In the current era, the tension is evident in the differences between President Trump, who emphasized American nationalism rather than the internationalism, which has characterized American foreign policy since 1945. Trump took a transactional approach to foreign affairs, in contrast to the traditional foreign policy establishment, which has believed in American leadership of international institutions and alliances. A remark by a recent American Secretary of State, Madeleine Albright, who called America "the indispensable country," encapsulated that view. In other words, without American leadership no major international initiative could be undertaken. For example, despite many European attempts to solve the upheavals in the Balkans in the 1990s, the issue was only resolved after the intervention of the United States.

That and many other events since the end of the Cold War in 1991 may be regarded as instances of international problems. But it became increasingly clear the world as a whole was being confronted with global problems, rather than those of the inter-state variety. These range from climate change, through the outbreak of disease epidemics, to financial and economic inequalities arising from economic globalization, to natural disasters, to pollution, to riverine questions and the distribution of water resources, and so on.

Arguably, at the core of these diverse problems is the absence of an institution that is global in scope with the authority – on occasion – to override the parochial interests of states. As things stand, the location of ultimate political authority remains within states whose legal sovereignty is absolute. The one major international body in existence, the United Nations, is an organization of states that, in practice, can only act with the consent of states, and its principal executive arm is the Security Council, where each of the five major powers can veto any proposed resolution. Therefore, any attempt to address problems of a global character requires the agreement of relevant states. Not only may state interests diverge and even conflict, governments of states may not even agree upon the nature of the problem or have the necessary capabilities to deal with it. The most egregious example is the government of former President Trump of the US, which disputed the scientific evidence that climate change is caused by human activities, and actually encouraged the further American development and production of carbon fuel on home ground. In any event, international agreements to limit the emission of greenhouse gases depend on voluntary actions by states to keep their commitments, and no provisions have so far been made to monitor, let alone enforce, their compliance.

The Endurance of Statehood

The issues posed by the existence of over 200 sovereign states with divergent and often conflicting interests in addressing problems which are global in nature go beyond those of an inter-state character. It should be borne in mind that statehood is the building block for the existence of international society as we currently recognize it, and as a means for institutionalizing relations between states. The rules, both formal and informal, which constitute that society are nearly all between states. Even those which are not, such as agreements between commercial companies or rules involving non-governmental organizations, are subject in the final analysis to regulation by sovereign states.

The beginnings of nationalism and modern statehood can be traced no further back than to the 17th and 18th centuries and are bound up with the beginnings of modernization, in the sense of industrialization, urbanization, mass literacy, the centralization of bureaucracy, and the emergence of citizenship and citizen armies. Nations which make up states are, in effect, bound by common rules, language, history, and political culture to regard the territorial confines of their respective states as setting the limits within which its members enjoy legitimate rights as a sovereign community. These developments undermined the previous political systems and empires, which were led by monarchs and aristocrats and composed of feudal rural communities, or serfdoms. By the 18ᵗʰ century, European sovereign states and nations became the primary focus of people's political loyalty. Governments of states alone were ensuring national security, and they were responsible for raising taxes, enacting binding laws, providing education at least to primary level and, in many cases, to the secondary level, the existence of a specialized work force for the construction and maintenance of appropriate infrastructure, and so on. Governments are expected to represent the citizens of states and to be accountable to them.

Nations differ from states in theory and in practice, although particular nations may be congruent with particular states. Nations, or those who claim to speak on their behalf, tend to claim to be based on common ethnic, cultural, linguistic, and historic identities of ancient origins. Such claims rarely stand up to careful historical research. Nevertheless, these nationalist claims tend to stir deep emotional support. Nationalism is also a means of separating one set of people from another, and it often gives rise to conflict between states, within states, and between different groupings claiming separate national identities.

International Agreements and Their Limits

States and nations tend to be jealous of their independence, which has constrained their attempts to establish enduring alliances, once their common enemy has ceased to be regarded as a major threat. They have found regional attempts to establish geographically based organizations have been subject to similar problems. Even the European Union, which has brought its member states and peoples into closer embrace than ever before, still found its attempt to establish a unified currency problematic as the relevant states could not establish the political institutions to undergird it. However, it has been possible to establish international agreements of global reach on particular, readily identifiable issues, which are seen to be in the universal interest. These include combatting infectious diseases, commercial international flight paths, the Universal Postal Union, and many more. But perhaps of particular interest is the Montreal Protocol of 1987, the first to limit and then rule out the use of particular chemicals and other ozone destroying substances in the earth's atmosphere. The preliminaries involved scientists and diplomats divided into small groups. The major developed countries concurred on the need to address the ozone 'holes' which had appeared over Antarctica. Provisions were made for less developed countries to take a longer time to adjust and even funds were established, care of a UN agency, to help the poorest countries.

As promising as the Montreal Protocol may appear, there were special circumstances facilitating its success. First, it addressed a narrowly focused issue. Second, it did not damage the interests of any of the great powers or any of their major manufacturing interests. Third, the technology for refrigeration (the main generator of the harmful gases) was already changing. Finally, the hole in the ozone layer was readily visible, and its elimination already enjoyed universal support. Similar points can be made about large-scale cross-border epidemics. By contrast, huge multivariate issues, such as climate change, touch on so many dimensions of life on earth that even when international agreement can be reached, say in the Paris Accord of November 2016, individual countries identified their particular commitments – implementation of which was to be entirely voluntary, and no agreement was reached on how to monitor compliance. Former President Trump of the United States (one of the world's major polluters) withdrew his country from the accord within days of his inauguration. In any case, major fossil energy producers found loopholes in the agreement and some of the key contributors to global warming such as China and India made limited commitments. Their governments could not overlook the pressing claims of their huge populations for further economic development.

Clearly the main responsibility of governments, especially of the democratic variety, is to safeguard the interests of their citizens. That necessarily involves having to mediate conflicting domestic interests, as well as to find ways of balancing immediate short term electorally popular interests with the longer-term ones. Consequently, it is very difficult to forge international agreements on matters involving major domestic interests of states. In that sense, states themselves and their domestic structures may be seen as principal sources of the difficulties in reaching binding international agreements on many issues of global significance. However, it is possible to conceive of alternative political governmental systems of a more global scope. But given the significance of nations and states, both for commanding emotional loyalty and for their scale in serving functional needs, it is not practical to propose the abolition of statehood – certainly not in time to address the manifold and immediate problems of climate change.

Possibly, a federation or confederation of states could be envisioned to encompass the world as a whole. States would continue to exist, but they would operate under the auspices of a wider global institution. However, even if a confederation were to be established so as to provide for the continued authority of separate states, there would first have to be agreement as to how to overcome the problems of delineating the authority and governance of each level of the confederation. Mechanisms would have to be established to settle disputes. The means of selecting leaders and to whom such leaders would be accountable would have to be found. The difficulties in reaching agreement about establishing such an institution are so formidable that nothing has yet been proposed that has been subject to serious consideration.

Given the urgency of addressing many of the current global problems and their inter-related character, it would seem the only means of doing so is through a series of inter-state agreements. In other words, there is no available alternative to states and their respective governments, if viable action is to be taken to address these problems – especially if their origins and development crisscross state boundaries. How to balance the interests of, say, South Asian countries in developing their economies to meet the current existential needs of their hundreds of millions of people, whose demands for cheap energy, clean water, modern infrastructure, etc., are immediate and rising, with those of other regions, who fear the effects of pollution and the release of global warming gas agents. In fact, the peoples of South Asia would be the first to suffer from economic development requiring the use of fossil fuel – yet there is no other immediate source of energy in sufficient volume and acceptable price to meet current demand. Another conundrum, for example, is how to balance the interests of those at the origins and heads of the mighty rivers that flow from the Tibetan plateau to south and southeast Asia. China controls these headwaters and it has an interest in building hydroelectric dams in order to produce clean energy, but in doing so China creates huge problems for those in neighboring countries down river. In a context in which powerful China is in a superior bargaining position, it is difficult to see how those living downstream could remedy their situation. It is possible different governments may be able to reach agreements with the Chinese side which could mitigate the situation, but, so far, China has resisted negotiations with the collectivity of relevant states, preferring instead to negotiate bilaterally with affected states – which of course strengthens its bargaining power still further.

China, of course, may be seen as the antithesis of cosmopolitanism. The Chinese Communist Party, especially under the leadership of Xi Jinping, emphasizes a parochial kind of nationalism, accentuating China's supposed grievances against the West and the United States. The traditional Communist call for proletarian internationalism has long since been abandoned. The current propaganda message is about restoring China's supposed past greatness. As for cosmopolitanism, I am reminded of an exchange I had with students and scholars of one of the institutes at the Chinese Academy of Social Science in 1978, shortly after it opened. I was asked about my identity, to which I responded by claiming to be a cosmopolitan. After I explained the concept, it became clear they or the scholars could not think of an equivalent in the Chinese language. The closest was "world-ist" (Shijie Zhuyizhe) which is not quite the same. If cosmopolitanism includes acceptance of diversity and empathy for others, that is not necessarily true of world-ism. World-ism may have divergent meanings, such as the aim for world government or for reducing and ultimately eradicating diversity, or it may call for varying degrees of conformity. In other words, it is inherently ambiguous, but it is further removed from the tolerance and empathy which are at the core of cosmopolitanism.

Nationalism and Cosmopolitanism

The new rise of nationalism in response to economic globalization, which has benefitted some countries at the expense of others and has increased inequalities within states, has intensified the difficulties in finding the means to address

152

problems, which are global in character, rather than a product of inter-state relations. At issue is how to generate a climate of opinion which would recognize and accept there are pressing global problems requiring global solutions in order to transcend the interests of states. That climate of opinion ideally should command intensity of emotional support, similar to the emotional loyalty generated by the nationalism of states.

The main means of expressing philosophical and emotional support for such a globalist approach is cosmopolitanism. Unfortunately, cosmopolitanism is associated with the dislocations linked to globalization, especially of the economic kind. Many attribute the recent emergence of populism allied with nationalism to the disruptive effects of globalization in the highly developed economies of North America and Europe, where many centers of manufacture have lost out to the cheaper producers of Asia, especially. That has been socially disruptive and has led many of the affected people to distrust established political institutions. In developed countries, the disruptions of globalization, aided by social media has led to greater polarization of people with conflicting views, between farming and urban interests, between the beneficiaries of higher education and the less-educated, and so on. At the same time, conflicts of interest have intensified between the developed and the less-developed countries. These disruptions to domestic and international order have caused people to draw into more narrowly conceived nation-based communities.

Not surprisingly, governments have paid more attention to national interests, and they have shown themselves to be less willing to expend resources on global issues, even though these, such as climate change, may be in the process of becoming more pressing. Typical is the response of the former British Prime Minister, Theresa May, who in no sense can be regarded as a populist. She once quipped, "if you believe you are a citizen of the world, you are a citizen of nowhere." It is precisely this viewpoint which undermines what may be regarded as relations with others, especially as we live in a world characterized by mutual interdependence. That entails not only mutual dependence, but also mutual obligations. Just as we will be aware of the implications for us of the actions of others, so we must take into consideration the effects of our actions upon them. Whether we like it or not, the peoples – as well as the economies of states – have become increasingly interdependent. In the world today, peoples have obligations to each other which go beyond those of citizenship in only one state.

Autarchy is not a viable option for any state, however richly it may be endowed. The citizens of every state benefit in due course from the discoveries and inventions made by citizens of other states. If the economies of states are to prosper, they need to engage in trade with others. Moreover, the rapid spread of communications has increased the interdependence of states and their citizens. At the same time, it is only by disregarding state borders the international community can address natural disasters, epidemics, and interstate wars that result in the breakdown of order and the plight of refugees. To these may be added the myriad consequences of climate change. The impact of these developments may be uneven between and within states, but in one way or another everyone is affected directly or indirectly. Considered from a global perspective, we are all citizens of the world, even though we do not have any documents to prove it, such as those of state citizens. In other words, even though the term 'citizen of the world' may be a metaphor, it encompasses a virtual reality that is becoming ever more visible.

Since retirement to the United States in 2003, my sense of the importance of the significance of looking at both national and international problems from a global perspective has been enhanced. It is precisely because the United States is the sole superpower, that its impact on the world is so great. Ironically, it was Former President Trump's emphasis on "America First", his attempt to disengage from alliances and multilateral obligations in his goal of reaching a balance of trade with all other countries, which actually demonstrated America's predominant weight in world affairs. No other country could threaten to destabilize the world's international systems to the extent the mercurial Trump achieved in his one term in office. It is true that in the process, Trump may have wrought fundamental damage to the United States both at home and abroad, but he has also demonstrated the unsurpassed power of America.

Trump has shown how America's "indispensability" can be used in a more disruptive way than Albright had in mind, by casting doubt on alliance obligations and more broadly on what has been called the "liberal international order". Both the positive and negative dimensions of America's predominance have brought to the fore the global character of the key elements of the major problems facing the world. Albright had in mind American leadership in addressing international problems, but Trump's approach involved a refusal to provide such leadership, and as a result there is a yawning gap in addressing many of these new and threatening global changes. These changes include, for example, demographic changes, technological inventions associated with Artificial Intelligence, the various huge ramifications of climate change – from the warming of polar regions and the consequent rise of sea levels to the heat inducing desertification, etc., etc., and the impact all of this will have on our way of life and especially on future generations.

This prospect is, or rather should be, perceived more clearly and keenly in the United States. At any rate, the sixteen years of my living in the United States have deepened my adherence to cosmopolitanism. According to the International Monetary Fund, the US still has the world's largest GDP, accounting for 22-25% of the world's GDP and is larger than that of its fellow members of the G7 (the world's most developed countries) combined. Even before the advent of the Trump presidency, the United States' ability to be an effective leader and protector of the world's liberal economic order was in decline. It was Trump's transactional approach to international trade, coupled with his unpredictability, that contributed to undermining that order still further. Arguably, it is only the relatively superior economic power of the United States, which allowed him to do so. To that may be added other aspects of American superior power: it is the world's major innovator of high technology. Its top universities and its postgraduate education are world leaders; it's military is superior to that of any other country; and its soft power is greater and more effective than any of its competitors. It is accustomed to leading world developments, and all other countries – friendly or otherwise – expect the US to exercise its superior power.

Even though most American citizens and many of their political representatives tend to be parochial in their outlook, their collective impact on the rest of the world is huge. The leaders of nearly all other countries seek to have their voices heard in Washington and strive to have their interests taken into account in American relevant policy-making. American elites are accustomed to playing leadership roles in addressing international problems as they arise and in trying to ensure that American interests are taken into account. As we have seen many international problems have morphed into global ones. Never before have so many global problems become so pressing and urgent, especially those linked to climate change.

Living in America as a fully-fledged citizen for more than 15 years has deepened the significance of the centrality of the United States in global affairs in my thinking about cosmopolitanism. Yet it is precisely at this point many countries have turned inwards in asserting a nationalism that denies obligations to others and which is divisive even at home. Perhaps one of the beneficial side effects of the coronavirus pandemic will be to impress upon peoples and their governments the significance of empathy and cooperation with others, as we are scheduled to confront increasing problems of a global character.

Conclusion

I shall argue by way of conclusion that the need for cosmopolitanism, or rather a cosmopolitan outlook, has never been greater than now. We live in a system of states, which militates against addressing collectively the pressing threats of global proportions. Indeed, the new rise of nationalism and populism makes collaboration between states, in order to identify and pursue common goals, even more difficult. The obstacles to changing the international system of separate sovereign states towards some kind of a world-wide confederation are immense, and they are unlikely to be overcome in the near future, let alone in time to meet the immanent global threats bearing down upon us. Hence, far from objecting to cosmopolitanism, we need to cultivate it to encourage deeper cooperation in the world in order to meet the emergent threats to global peace and prosperity and as a means to overcome the current focus on parochial state and national interests. A positive move in that direction is the worldwide movement of young people to challenge their elders and existing governments to implement policies to arrest climate change. Young people from scores of countries, including those under immediate threat and from the less developed to the highly developed, have coordinated their protests and activities across continents. They have included indigenous people – from the Arctic to hot arid lands – to address the developed world in demanding that the damage to their environment, caused mainly by the industrialized countries, be reversed. Those demanding the problems of climate change be addressed may not directly espouse cosmopolitanism, but the underlying principles of their activism transcend state boundaries and parochial interests – all of which lie at the core of cosmopolitanism.

As earlier chapters have outlined, my experiences as a youth and a young man sowed within me the outlook of a cosmopolitan, even though I was not aware of the concept and its ramifications. As a young academic, I began to appreciate some of the attributes of cosmopolitanism, and, as I matured as an academic and a student of China, I realized the significance of both its universal values and the empathy it made possible for different cultures. To do so involved understanding different points of view, without giving up one's own or declining into pointless relativism, in which no distinctions could be drawn between the values people held. Moreover, in the Post-Cold-War era, I began to sense the dangers facing the world were less those of inter-state warfare but rather those of a global character.

As suggested earlier, there is a mismatch between our system of states and the global character of the threats we need to address. The peoples of the world are divided by separate nation-states, each with a government whose main legal and moral responsibility is to meet the needs of its citizens within the geographical boundaries of the state. For their part, citizens are expected to be loyal to the state and its principal nation. In so far as states have international obligations beyond their geographical boundaries these are set by such treaties and legal agreements reached with other states and those laid out in international law, which lack the enforcement mechanisms of domestic or municipal law and which is therefore observed on a voluntary basis as dependent on the relative power of states and the degree of their attachment to their international standing as reputable states.

With the threat of a general war between the major states receding, the principal threat to the safety of citizens of states is global or universal in character. The most pressing such threat derives from climate change in its various manifestations. Unlike previous existential threats, which were derived mainly from economic or military rivalry between states, climate change has a regional and a global character that affects states but is not derived from inter-state relations. The effects of climate change may be seen right now in increasing heat waves, in the growing intensity of storms, in the rise of sea levels, in water shortages, changes in crop cultivation, the melting of ice in the polar regions and in high mountain ranges, riverine changes, and so on. The latter involves changes in river flows, separating the interest of those upstream from those downstream. For example, most of the major rivers of Asia emanate from the Tibetan Himalayan plateau, and China is in the process of building dams in the upper reaches of these rivers. The building of these dams is to mitigate the effects of climate change through the use of hydro-electricity instead of fossil fuel to generate much needed electricity in China. However laudable the Chinese activities maybe for mitigating the impact of climate change, the repercussions for states and communities downstream, which have already experienced major disruptions to the Mekong River on which much of their livelihood depended, have been in many cases disastrous. Fishing communities have been disrupted, and the supply of fish to the region cutback, with ill effects on the millions for whom fish has been the main source of protein. The supply of fresh water to the river's delta has been reduced, causing more of the area to be inundated with seawater and damaging the soil for farming. Similar riverine issues are occurring in regions already subject to political and military conflict and instability, including the Middle East and South Asia, with even fewer prospects of a resolution.

Developments such as these, allied to the breakdown of order in many less developed states, have already led to massive flows of refugees to the more developed states, which are increasingly unable or unwilling to absorb them. The international agreements and laws devised in an earlier era to deal with refugees and asylum seekers are no longer being observed under current conditions. In other words, issues related to climate change are already weakening the utility of existing international laws and agreements.

Inter-state agreements have been reached in the 21st century to try and limit the further heating of the earth beyond 2 degrees Centigrade, but these agreements are of limited utility, because there is no agreed universal formula for limiting the discharge of harmful gases produced by fossil fuel, leaving each state to determine its own discharges. There is also no mechanism for enforcing even these self-selected limits. In December 2015, all the more than 200 states in the world reached an accord to reduce the harmful gases they discharge into the atmosphere, but the major dischargers set different criteria for measuring the harmful products, and no arrangements were made for independent monitoring of the results. Even so, the Trump administration unilaterally withdrew the United States from the

Paris accord only two months after it was signed, thereby casting doubt on the efficacy of the agreement.

Unfortunately, the general climate of opinion in many parts of the world, and especially in the more liberal and democratic countries of Europe and North America, has turned against the global values and institutions which had previously underpinned the international order established in the aftermath of the Second World War. It is especially troubling that those who might have been expected to take a lead in turning back the tide of populist, narrow nationalism, such as the previous British Prime Minister, Theresa May, who, as the daughter of a Church of England clergyman and as an upholder of traditional English middle-class values, (as noted earlier) unprompted dismissed cosmopolitan values wholesale.

Cosmopolitan values, after all, are at the core of all the major religions and are embedded deep in the cultures and viewpoints of many of the world's peoples. These include respect for strangers and tolerance for opinions other than ones own. The biblical injunction to "love thy neighbor as thyself" is well known. Less well known, is the insistence by Confucius, "Do not impose on others what you yourself do not desire" and "Love your fellow men". There is a well-known statement by the prophet Mohammed, made during his stay in Medina, "to you be your religion, to me be mine". His constitution from that period demanded that all religious groups be protected. The same is true for Buddhism and other major regions. To be sure, intolerant groups of believers can be found in most religions, both in opposition to others within the same religion as well as to believers in other religions. But that does not detract from the point that important cosmopolitan values can be observed in the mainstream texts of all the major religions. Indeed, far from being an alien or a modern concoction, adherence to cosmopolitanism was explicitly advocated by the "cynics" and "stoics" in ancient Greece and Rome. It was the Emperor Ashoka of the 4th and 3rd centuries B "I' before "CE in India who was the first to introduce the principle of non-violence into International Relations.

It is true that the cosmopolitan emphasis on values which are universal does not in principle accord with the cosmopolitan celebration of difference, but, in practice, the incompatibility of the two values may not be so apparent. For example, much would depend on how universality and difference are defined and understood. Universality need not mean regarding all values as equally valid or rather being unable to distinguish between their relative validity. For example, respecting strangers and tolerating diverse opinions does not mean it is necessary to like and to befriend all strangers, nor does tolerance for diverse opinions mean it is necessary to agree with all of them; it means strangers should not be rejected or shunned and opinions found disagreeable should be given a hearing and the reasons for disagreement presented in a civil way.

The principal idea of cosmopolitanism is that all human beings regardless of their political affiliations are members of a single global community. According to the Stanford Encyclopedia of Philosophy, different versions of this community can be found among cosmopolitans. Some focus on political institutions, others on moral norms or relationships, and still others share forms of cultural expression. All the different versions, however, agree we all share a common global community. It is one thing to identify the global community in theory, but it is quite another to demonstrate its existence in practice.

Although it is possible to argue the potential for such a community exists, it is yet to be realized. Further, even if it is arguably in the process of developing, recognition of a community spanning the globe is highly unlikely to come into fruition in the near future, let alone to emerge in time to meet the challenges of climate change, which are already evident. The era of globalization from the 1990s to the middle of the second decade of the 21ˢᵗ century is currently in disarray. The rise of China has undermined the previous norms and practice of international trade, the developed world has lost much of its industrial manufacturing, in part due to the advances of automation, but also to the transfer of much manufacturing to China and the developing countries of Asia. Combined with other factors, the result has been the impoverishment of the traditional working class of North America and much of Western Europe and the disruption of their social order. The disillusion with the democratic institutions has found expression in the re-emergence of populism and a nationalism based on a sense of grievance about the deepening divide between the bulk of the people and a thin layer of those who have benefited greatly from economic globalization.

As for China, its stance as the main upholder of globalization after Trump's withdrawal from the Paris Agreements of climate change and his objections to multilateralism is delusory. Despite China being the principal beneficiary of globalization, China pursues policies of mercantilism at the expense of less developed countries as well as the most developed. Its nationalism is based on a sense of grievance against Western countries and Japan, and its international outlook and behavior is very much focused on its own interests – to the exclusion of consideration for those of others. Its dealings with the rest of the world may be summarized as being based on the expectation that foreigners should familiarize themselves with China and its culture without the Chinese, on the whole, being expected to be interested in foreign countries and their cultures. That was not true of Chinese intellectuals in the first half of the 20ᵗʰ century, but since the consolidation of communist power in the 1950s China, has become the least cosmopolitan of the major powers.

In the context of these developments in the West and in the leading Asian power and its supporters, the tide of opinion is unlikely to favor the ideas associated with cosmopolitanism, yet the challenges posed especially by climate change require a common approach by the world as a whole, even though the international system of nation-states is a major obstacle to such a unified approach. Cosmopolitanism, or even just elements of it which recognize the obligations of every political community towards others, would offer a principle on which such challenges could be approached. The adoption of cosmopolitan approaches would also conform to the key goal of Realism – self-survival. But from now on it would require the transcendence of sovereign statehood to embrace new issues requiring regional or global solutions.

As noted earlier, the emergence of the worldwide movement of young people to challenge existing governments and international institutions may be seen as an example of a cosmopolitan outlook in practice. They have coordinated their activities, which stretch across the many complex manifestations of climate change as they have appeared in their own localities. Examples stretch from the melting of the ice in the polar regions to the desertification of semi-arid areas, from the burning of huge tropical forests to the intensification of storms. The effects lead to huge water shortages in some parts of the world and to excessive flooding in others; they also lead to disputes over riverine sources. As regions become uninhabitable, the numbers of migrating peoples increase, and the resistance of others to accommodate them also increases. In short, cosmopolitanism has been transformed from an affectation by privileged urban dwellers, to a cause of immediate concern to all peoples.

166

Biden still faces formidable difficulties in trying to enact the agenda he put forward in the course of the election. To be sure, the Republicans, under the leadership of Senator McConnell, confront President Biden with the kind of obstructions faced by President Obama, which forces Biden to rely on Presidential Executive actions – with the additional difficulties of dealing with an unsympathetic judiciary headed by the Supreme Court.

The Biden administration has been faced by a number of dilemmas from the outset. For example, in order to restore "tolerance and decency" at home, with respect for minorities and democracy under the law, will the administration seek to take to court officials from the outgoing administration, including perhaps Trump, even if doing so would create a dangerous precedent of a new administration punishing its predecessor? Or on a different issue, how far should the Biden administration go and how quickly to proceed in moves to facilitate greater economic equality? How would the priorities of government spending be determined in dealing with heath care, educational needs and the building of infrastructure in addition to a wide variety of social needs? The administration also seeks to improve socio-political norms by favoring public service over the exclusive pursuit of private advantage.

Perhaps carrying out a new foreign policy would face fewer difficulties. The Biden administration could be expected to rejoin the international institutions from which Trump withdrew. More broadly, multilateralism would be preferred to unilateral actions and support for the main principles of foreign policy that prevailed before Trump became president. Biden will seek to restore alliances and seek to build trust through pursuing a more consist foreign policies in which attention will be paid to upholding human rights. However, it will be necessary to adjust to the new international environment, including particularly the question of the rise of mercantilist

China and its growing power with its attempt to bully neighbors and reduce America's influence in the Asia-Pacific. President Biden has indicated he will avoid treating China as an enemy, but there will be no return to Obama's balanced engagement policies. Instead, there will be a policy combining areas of cooperation, such as on climate change, pandemics, etc., with areas of competition on strategic issues in the maritime domains such as those in the East and South China Seas. They include Taiwan and the islands controlled by Japan as well as freedom of civil and military passage through the South China Sea. The possible use of force would depend on Chinese actions.

The Biden administration has indicated it will not necessarily remove the tariffs Trump imposed on China. Again, much will depend on China's behavior with regard to trade, i.e., bringing to an end its discriminatory treatment of foreign trade entities and ending its practice of stealing secret technological innovations, etc., from foreign companies and entities. In addition, if obstructions of investment and economic activities by foreign enterprises should continue economic cooperation would be limited.

To conclude, in order to address these issues, as well as the complex challenges of climate change, the re-building of infrastructure, reform of education, improving health care, and so on, a change of culture can be expected to emerge over time for the emphasis to shift from private gain to public good – perhaps as encouraged during the era of Presidents Kennedy and Johnson. Regardless, the success of Biden's broad aims are clearly more favorable to what may be called the Cosmopolitan project than anything associated with Trump.

A Biden administration would seem to restore international trust in America as a force for observing international law, norms, and treaties. Multilateral institutions would be rejoined, and American obligations to them would be honored.

But much depends on the Democratic Party majority in the Senate. Otherwise, Biden and his party would face considerable resistance – and even obstruction – in their attempts to introduce new legislation and new cultural norms of tolerance. However, Biden's administration will encounter considerable difficulty in undoing the 'damage' done by Trump and his cabinet. For example, how would the concern to establish 'decency' and 'tolerance' be balanced with the perceived need to bring the lawbreakers of the previous administration to account? And would there be concern for setting a precedent for new administrations in the treatment of their predecessors? Leaving aside the administrative and political difficulties that would have to be overcome in reversing many of the executive orders and laws passed by the Trump administration, a Biden administration would encounter an unsympathetic Supreme Court in dealing with much of the new legislation and executive orders that would inevitably enlarge the scope of government, whether to address the complex challenges of climate change, or to carry out the commitment of Biden to build new and restore old infrastructure and more generally to change the culture of the country from the emphasis of private gain to public good. Whether or not President Biden will succeed in his broad aims, they are clearly more favorable to the Cosmopolitan project than anything associated with Trump.

Appendix A

Yahuda Family Tree

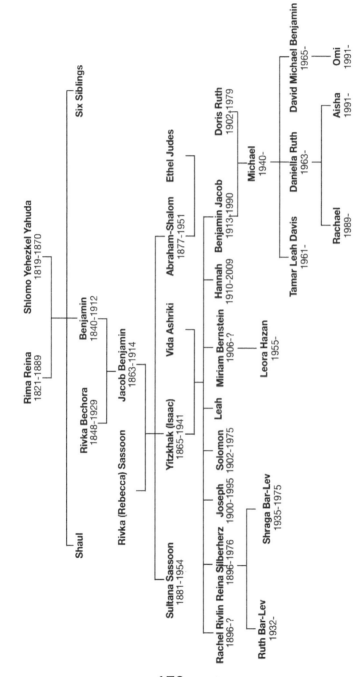

Appendix B

Notes on Various Family Members

On my father's side:

Shlomo Yehezkel Yahuda (1819-1871) Married **Rima Reina (1821-1889).** It was he who left the family of the House of Yahuda (Judah) in Baghdad for Jerusalem in 1853. He founded there a Yeshiva (Jewish Seminary) named Hessed El and bought land in Motsa, 5 miles/8 kilometers west of the old city of Jerusalem, which the family farmed. Shlomo (Solomon) was also the first member of his Baghdadi/Sephardi family to marry an Ashkenazi. Rima was the daughter of the distinguished Bechora family of Vienna. Part of her wedding trousseau has been passed down to me: a wedding bed cover woven in silk, with indigo and gold threads, and pillow and cushions to match.

Shaul Yehezkel Yahuda (1840-1864). Family lore has it he caught pneumonia by riding through a storm from Motsa to Jerusalem to make the family Sabbath on time. There is a hill on what used to be the outskirts of Jerusalem named after him, called Givat Shaul. He had six other siblings.

Benjamin Yehzkel Yahuda (1839-1912). Son of Shlomo, was a leader of the influential Baghdadi Jewish community in Jerusalem.

Yitzhak Yehezkel Yahuda (1865-1941) married **Vida Ashriki.** Yitzhak, my grandfather, was a distinguished scholar of Hebraica and Arabica, who corresponded with scholars world wide (including the **Vatican**), and was also a consultant on Islamic Law at the premier Islamic university, Al Azhar, in

Cairo. He was a buyer and seller of rare manuscripts and was also the compiler and commentator of Arabian Proverbs in three volumes. Isaac is the English equivalent of Yitzhak. Yitzhak had nine children, beginning with Rachel and continuing with Reina, Joseph, Solomon, Leah, Miriam, Hannah and Benjamin(my father).

Abraham-Shalom Yahuda (1877-1951) married **Edith Jahanes** from South Africa, **Abraham-Shalom** was a world famous Scholar of Semitic Studies and was a public intellectual. Among his friends were Freud and Einstein. He was appointed the first professor of Semitic Studies by King Alphonso XIII of Spain. He was a teacher, researcher, writer, and collector of rare books. At the time of his death, he had a library of manuscripts and incunabula that, in addition to Jewish and Moslem manuscripts, also included the religious manuscripts of Isaac Newton, some letters of Napoleon, etc. In 1952 the library was valued at $1.5 million (in 2021 US$ at least 15 million). He was an ardent promoter of a Jewish state in the land of Israel. He attended the first five World Jewish Congresses, but he criticized the Zionist leaders for focusing on the European dimension of Judaism to the neglect of the rich cultural legacy of Spanish (i.e., Andalusian) Jewry which, together with their Arab hosts, had helped lay the foundation for the emergence of modernity. Its contemporary significance was in demonstrating a profound example of how Jews and Arabs could live together to mutual advantage. Abraham Shalom wrote many books and was honored with a state burial by Israel.

Michael Benjamin Yahuda (b.1940) Professor Emeritus, the London School of Economics. His children are **Tamar Davis (b. 1961,) Daniella Yahuda (b. 1963)** and **David Yahuda (b. 1965).**

Daniella has two daughters, **Rachel (b.1989)** and **Aisha (b.1991). David** has one daughter, **Omi Feeney (b.1991)**

On my mother's side:

Thomas Henry Tankard (1854-1932) arrived aged 2 in one of the four sailing ships that contributed to the founding of Christchurch New Zealand. He became the country's leading cornet player and led a band for many years.

Judge Peter Mahon (1925-1986) As a High Court Judge, he chaired the Commission of Inquiry which investigated the crash of Air New Zealand in 1979 on Mount Erebus, in Antarctic. He called the airline's attempt to blame the pilot with concocted explanations, "a litany of lies'. Initially, he was subject to much criticism by the NZ authorities including Prime Minister Maldoon. He was fully exonerated after his death, and his method of conducting the inquiry has been widely adopted.

Sam Mahon, (b. 1954) the son of the judge, has become a famous artist in his own right and a prominent critic of the local South Island authorities' policies, which damage the Canterbury Plain.

Appendix C

Listed family names in order of appearance

My father's family:

(Prof.) Abraham Shalom Yahuda, 1877-1951 (the uncle) p. 11; 12; 21; 23; 36; 38; 45; 149

Joseph Yahuda, 1900-1995 (lawyer; my father's oldest brother) p. 22; 39; 41-44; 149

Isaac (Yitzhak) Yehezkel Yahuda, 1866-1941 (my grandfather) p. 12; 20; 36-37; 148

Solomon Yahuda, 1902-1975 (lawyer; my father's older brother) p. 26; 39; 41; 149

Reina Zilberherz, née Yahuda, 1896-1976 (my father's oldest surviving sister) p. 26; 39-40; 42; 148

Sultana Sassoon, née Yahuda, 1881-1954 (my father's aunt) p. 36; 38; 149

Miriam Bernstein, née Yahuda (my father's sister), b.1906 p. 39-40; 149

Chaim Zilberherz (husband of Reina), 1896-1977 p. 35; 39-40; 41

Hannah Braun, née Yahuda, 1910-2009 (my father's sister) p. 39-41; 43-44; 149

Shraga Bar-Lev, 1935-1975 (son of Reina and Chaim) p. 39-40

Ruthie Bar-Lev (daughter of Reina and Chaim), b.1932 p. 39-41

Naomi Nissim (wife of Solomon) p. 41

My mother's family, New Zealand:

Thomas Tankard, 1854-1932 (my grandfather) arrived aged two on one of "the four sailing ships" from Yorkshire, UK, in 1856 that contributed to the founding of Christchurch, South Island, N.Z. He became NZ's premier cornet player and led a well-known band. p. 78; 149

High Court Judge Peter Mahon, 1923-1986(my mother's nephew) in 1979 he headed the Judicial Inquiry into the Air New Zealand 'plane that had crashed into Mount Erebus in Antarctica. He reversed the Airline's judgment, supported by the Prime Minister a pilot's error caused the crash and blamed it on the airline, which he said presented a "litany of lies". The Judge was pilloried by the authorities, but was exonerated in the end, unfortunately after his early death at the age of 62. His inquiry was later to serve as a model for other airlines. p. 78; 150

Sam Mahon, 1958 (the son of the judge) is a famous artist and environmentalist. p. 78; 150